ADVANCE PRAISE

"A powerful resource for all of us who are deeply invested in the pursuit of excellence and peak performance, whether in business or in life. I will be recommending Live Empowered! for my colleagues and loved ones seeking to remove mysterious roadblocks in their life."

—PIERS CAREY, CEO, TENEO, LTD.

"A must-read for those invested in true mind and body wellness, as well as performing at our very best. Hard to put down."

—MARSHA RALLS, UNITED NATIONS AMBASSADOR FOR WOMEN'S ENTREPRENEURSHIP DAY, FOUNDER, CEO, THE PHOENIX WELLNESS RETREAT

"A brave exploration of new thinking and tools by a neuro-psychologist willing to give it all to empower her patients."

—ALVARO FERNANDEZ, CEO, EDITOR-IN-CHIEF, SHARPBRAINS, COAUTHOR, *THE SHARPBRAINS GUIDE TO BRAIN FITNESS*

"As an adopted woman that has struggled her whole life with implicit memories, I am so grateful to Dr. Julie for writing this much-needed book and sharing her work so that she continues to help other adopted people and those struggling with trauma. How thrilling that there really is a way to move forward and that these wounds do not have to hold us hostage for a lifetime."

—ZARA PHILLIPS, AUTHOR, *SOMEBODY'S DAUGHTER*

"I thought I was reading *Live Empowered!* with an eye toward how my implicit memories could be affecting my personal relationships, but I found myself constantly applying the lessons to my business life as well. As a small business owner and entrepreneur, there is virtually no distance between those two aspects of my life, and it was so fascinating that as I explored this book, the applications had an impact on my total life— not just one side or the other."

—JENNIFER ADELI, CEO, WINBIZ PROPOSALS

"*Live Empowered!* is life-changing in its ability to dramatically improve the quality of daily living. Beautifully written and able to be immediately applied. This book is also filled with critical information that is essential for any practitioners working with trauma, whether it be physical or emotional. Bravo!"

—LISA KLEIN, CEO, FOUNDER, TOTAL HEALTH PHYSICAL THERAPY

"A great resource for anyone interested in understanding the power and promise of changing implicit memory. I appreciate Julie's candor in sharing the importance of EMDR therapy in her own healing, inspiring others to have the courage to take the journey themselves. Live Empowered! is an easy-to-follow guide on a complex topic, which is difficult to accomplish. Brilliant."

—DEANY LALIOTIS, DIRECTOR OF TRAINING, EMDR INSTITUTE, CODIRECTOR, EMDR OF GREATER WASHINGTON, DC

"Dr. Julie Lopez has created an incredible body of work! She has finally demystified implicit memory by providing an accessible pathway to understanding what drives reactions that are out of awareness. Furthermore, she gives concrete information about three vital brain-based therapies allowing those who suffer with trauma, tangible options for a way forward and real hope for changing what seemed impossible to change."

—MONICA FREEDMAN, FACULTY, GEORGE WASHINGTON UNIVERSITY MEDICAL SCHOOL, NEUROFEEDBACK/TRAUMA THERAPIST

"*Live Empowered! powerfully describes a truth about the human system—that our preverbal experiences lay down invisible yet hardwired patterns of coping; and such patterns, which once may have been valuable, can later sabotage our forward movement in life. What is beautiful is that these patterns become malleable with brain-based therapies. As a naturopathic physician and master energy healer, I fully believe our bodies are self-healing, and addressing the obstacles blocking our innate healing force is a critical component of my work. I enjoy working on a deep level with my clients, and I am so excited to have all of this rich information at my fingertips to support them in their healing and growth.*"

—DR. MARIE RODRIGUEZ, NATUROPATHIC PHYSICIAN

"*I'm thrilled that Dr. Julie Lopez has written an invaluable guide for any of us who want to move beyond the limitations of past traumatic events and realize our full potential. Dr. Julie makes complicated brain science easy to understand, with inspiring examples of healing drawn from her therapy practice and from her own life. As a psychologist, I strongly recommend Live Empowered! as a resource for clients, and also for fellow clinicians seeking a rich and comprehensive book on brain-based therapies.*"

—DR. MICHAEL RADKOWSKY, CLINICAL PSYCHOLOGIST

LIVE EMPOWERED!

LIVE EMPOWERED!

REWIRE YOUR BRAIN'S IMPLICIT MEMORY TO THRIVE IN BUSINESS, LOVE, AND LIFE

DR. JULIE LOPEZ

LIONCREST
PUBLISHING

LIVE EMPOWERED!
Rewire Your Brain's Implicit Memory to
Thrive in Business, Love, and Life

ISBN   978-1-5445-1390-4 *Paperback*
       978-1-5445-1389-8 *Ebook*

This book is dedicated to my people.

Not those of my heritage,

*But rather those without say or consent on
the drastic U-turns of their lives,*

U-turns that cause invisible ruptures but countless visible symptoms.

CONTENTS

"The horrors of war, pale beside the loss of a mother."

—ANNA FREUD

INTRODUCTION

THE BEGINNING OF A PASSION

I was in my early twenties, living on my own, and learning how to be an adult. One night as I was making dinner, a grease fire erupted in my kitchen. I had never seen a grease fire before, so instinctively, I threw water on it, not knowing that would only cause the fire to explode and spread across the kitchen. For a brief moment, I wondered: Was I going to die?

Fortunately, after a few tense moments, I managed to get the blaze under control. My kitchen had mostly survived—and so had I—but the experience left me feeling powerless and overwhelmed.

For weeks, that feeling stayed with me. Everywhere I

went, my body remained on high alert. The feeling got so bad that I couldn't even get through a simple conversation about the experience without tearing up. Consciously, I knew I was safe, but something in my system didn't agree.

With the help of my therapist, I started putting the pieces of my story together. On the one hand, I knew the story of what had happened to me: the fire, the helplessness, and the fear that consumed me.

On the other hand, I didn't understand how the experience had affected me on a sensory level. The sight of the fire, the heat in the kitchen, the smell of burning objects, the sound of the explosion—all of these sensory inputs had encoded a message in my human system—a message without words that continued to overwhelm me long after the event had passed.

I hadn't died, of course, and consciously, I understood that. However, the mere act of telling this story to friends and family would trigger visceral reactions consistent with those of a person experiencing distress, causing a sudden rush of sensory experiences that left me feeling overwhelmed and helpless all over again.

Two Types of Knowing

1) Intellectual/Logical Knowing

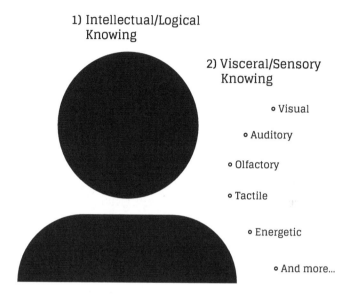

2) Visceral/Sensory Knowing

- Visual
- Auditory
- Olfactory
- Tactile
- Energetic
- And more...

THE DISCONNECT

Sometimes, we experience a disconnect between how we believe we should respond to a situation and how we actually respond. When this happens, we're often left feeling embarrassed at our reaction—ashamed of being "oversensitive," "touchy," "impulsive," or any other of a range of negative labels. Sometimes, we don't want to respond the way we do, but we can't help it. It's as if a secret, internal code was written into our systems to make us respond that way.

Such behavior-influencing "codes" wield even more power

in the wake of a major distressing event or life challenge. Someone involved in a bicycle crash, for instance, might not be surprised to find that in the months following the crash, the mere sight of a bicycle causes some degree of stress. Rationally, the cyclist knows the bike doesn't pose a threat. However, somewhere inside, their system is feeding them a different message—one that a bike is a signal of danger (Bike = Danger). They don't intellectually believe that, since they have been cycling for decades. Somewhere in their body, however, this new code has formed.

Even when we experience challenges that are relatively minor, this same internal coding process takes place, though the results are usually far subtler. For instance, when I was telling the story of my kitchen fire to a friend, he started to playfully tease me. His behavior wasn't anything serious. It was just the kind of gentle ribbing anyone could expect from a friend after a somewhat stressful experience. I understood this intellectually. However, emotionally, I was at the whims of an internal saboteur I didn't—and couldn't—understand.

"What's your problem?" I shouted at him, not being able to contain my reaction. "Why do you have to be such a jerk about everything?"

My friend was taken aback, but I didn't care. At the time, I felt fully justified in my response. However, upon reflection, I realized I had overreacted. It was obvious that my friend had been trying to make me feel better, and he couldn't have known I would respond so negatively. However, my system still hadn't caught up with the reality of the situation. I was furious and unable to connect my reaction to the deep-seated response that the fire had triggered in me. As a result, I took action in words and tone, and I called my friend a jerk.

I didn't want to be angry. I didn't want to break down in tears at the mere thought of the fire, either. The experience was over, so why couldn't I escape the shadow it was casting over my behavior?

Perhaps in your life you have experienced something similar. Have you ever been surprised by your reaction to a particular experience? Have you ever had a moment where, intellectually, you *knew* that whatever you were experiencing was no big deal, but your body was sending a different signal? Or have you ever been confused at your struggle or even outright resistance to doing something that you really *wanted* to do for no obvious reason?

If so, then perhaps, like me, you had become a prisoner of your own *implicit memories*. As I learned, if I was going to move forward, I needed a way to access those memories and change my responses toward situations that triggered them.

WHAT IS IMPLICIT MEMORY?

In simple terms, our minds are divided into two main areas: the conscious and the unconscious. The conscious mind of your hippocampus and frontal lobe are home to what is called *explicit memory*, or the experiences and memories we can easily recall.[1] The unconscious mind, on the other hand, contains a vast reservoir of data commonly known as *implicit memory*, or all the experiences, memories, and knowledge we've built up over the natural course of our lives but can't, or don't, consciously access.[2]

To develop a sense of how our human system processes and stores data, consider the lives of babies. Though precognitive and preverbal, babies spend the first parts of their lives taking in the world through a variety of experiences and sensory data. While we have no direct conscious access to this data later in our lives, studies show it nevertheless has a profound impact on our development. For instance, a study by the Harvard Center on the Developing Child found a direct correlation between preconscious experiences and developmental and performance outcomes later in life.[3] Quite literally, the

---

1   Eric R. Kandel and Sarah Mack, *Principles of Neural Science*, 5th ed. New York: McGraw-Hill Medical, 2013).

2   Kim Ann Zimmerman, "Implicit Memory: Definition and Examples," *Live Science*, February 12, 2014, https://www.livescience.com/43353-implicit-memory.html.

3   National Scientific Council on the Developing Child, "Children's Emotional Development Is Built into the Architecture of Their Brains" (working paper no. 2., 2004), https://developingchild.harvard.edu/wp-content/uploads/2004/04/Childrens-Emotional-Development-Is-Built-into-the-Architecture-of-Their-Brains.pdf.

ability to process emotions, learn how to identify emotions in others, empathize, and tolerate strong emotion are all cornerstones for functioning later in life and are greatly influenced by memories created before we become conscious.

Often, the way we process these implicit memories is to our benefit. A highly sophisticated supercomputer, the human system is constantly seeking ways to grow and improve, and it draws from our implicit memories to create positive connections that enable us to learn from our mistakes and try again. However, while our human system is always creating adaptive associations that help us in the moment, sometimes these very same associations can later become barriers to meeting our goals in our everyday lives.

THE HIDDEN CONTROL PANEL

This was the case for me and my responses to the grease fire. Every time I thought back to that incident, the memory triggered a strong response that I didn't understand and couldn't consciously control: an elevated heart rate, tightening in the throat, extra energy in my arms and legs, and anxiety. While engaging in traditional talk therapy, my therapist suggested a different type of treatment: Eye Movement Desensitization and Reprocessing (EMDR) to help me process my experience with the fire on a different level.

Through this approach, he explained, we would gain more direct access to a hidden control panel in my brain, target the parts of my experience of the grease fire housed in my implicit memory system, and reprogram my response to them. This metaphorical and invisible type of control panel lives in our unconscious, and in my case, it provided signals to my body to raise my heart rate, produce adrenaline, and jump into action to survive the fire. Those signals were now ongoing and influencing my aggression towards my friend and bodily experience of distress at the slightest reminder of the fire.

I wasn't exactly sure what my therapist was proposing. In fact, the whole thing sounded pretty weird to me. However, I trusted him, so I agreed to give the process a try. During the session, I felt something change inside me and began to relate to my experience differently. The next day, for the first time since the incident, I could talk about the fire without tearing up. I even laughed at my friends' jokes about burning down the house.

That experience marked the beginning of my experience with brain-based therapies. I had seen firsthand that there was indeed a hidden control panel in my brain, and I understood that by learning to access it and reprogram it in a pointed way, I could more rapidly improve my life and the lives of others.

Since earning my PhD in clinical social work, I have made implicit memory my life's work. I know what it's like to feel out of control with your emotional, physical, and relational reactions and not understand why—and not just because of the grease fire explosion. Throughout this book, you will learn a little bit about the story of my own rough start to life, being given up for adoption and my time in an orphanage, and how undergoing this therapeutic work has made possible profound changes in my own well-being. More importantly, I know how freeing it can be to find something that works—sometimes in as little as one session—and dramatically change your day-to-day experience. Now at the Viva Center, my mental health center in Washington, DC, I have designed numerous programs and trained a fleet of clinicians all with one purpose: to help clients live empowered lives.

You can't change what you aren't aware of—no matter how well you might educate yourself on different therapeutic techniques. Naturally, this can be frustrating, which is why countless clients often come to me saying, "Why can't I solve this myself?" We may want to, but if the core obstacle is tucked away in implicit memory, you simply cannot fix it on your own.

For some clients, their life goals are both discrete and within reach—a woman looking for more intimacy with her partner, a manager seeking to effectively support her staff, or a marathon runner trying to improve his performance. Often, targeting and reprocessing the roadblocks that keep clients from such achievements can be accomplished in only a few sessions.

For other clients, their roadblocks have become so pervasive that they have had a profound negative impact on their lives. Recently, I began working with a man who had developed a sensory eating disorder early in life that had followed him into early middle age. A smart, proactive man, this client had read countless books and visited dozens of experts but had been unable to arrive at a solution. The best anyone could offer were strategies to manage his difficulties. By the time he came to me, he was tired of the constant shame this disorder had caused. He didn't want to manage his symptoms. He wanted to eliminate them.

Through a series of EMDR sessions, we opened up the control panel in his brain (his implicit memory system) and began to unpack the layers of implicit memories associated with this disorder. Soon, we had remapped his body's response to eating. The contractions and the physical tension he was holding in his lower and upper intestines and his vagus nerve were gone. What was once unthinkable for this client—eating in public, attending social events, even going on dates—had now become possible. While this client and I had more work to do, he was off to a great start.

TAKE CONTROL

Most of my clients at the Viva Center don't know about implicit memory or how advanced brain- or body-based therapies can be used to retarget our psychological and physical responses in very productive ways. By the time they come to the center, they've all but given up hope. They've tried other doctors, they've tried medication, they've tried a variety of medical and psychological approaches focused on symptom management, and nothing has worked. They're tired of feeling trapped. They're tired of being misdiagnosed, mistreated, and pathologized when in reality, their minds are simply trying to adapt to a past circumstance that was hard on their system. A code has been written into their hidden control panel, and although they can't see that code, their lives are being sabotaged as a result of it.

If these experiences resonate with your own, this book can help you take control of your life. Therapies effective at healing implicit memory give you the power to access the hidden control panel in your mind, address the root causes of your roadblocks, and reprogram your responses—often in a fraction of the time it would take through classical psychological methods.

In the following chapters, I am going to show you how the mind works, how it processes and stores vast amounts of data on the subconscious level, and how you can access and reconfigure that data by accessing the implicit memory system in your mind. While in reality, the instrument for accessing our unconscious is far more complex than a simple control panel, I have chosen to describe it this way to make the science of implicit memory–based therapies accessible without going too heavily into the jargon associated with them.

Each of the following chapters explores the processes of our mind's hidden control panel in detail. Before we discuss those, however, let's first establish the basics of how brain- or body-based therapy works and how we will be discussing it for the purposes of this book.

UNDERSTANDING BRAIN- OR BODY-BASED THERAPY

Brain-based therapy emerged from the larger study of neuropsychology—the study of how the brain and the rest of the nervous system influence people's thoughts and behaviors. Central to this work are the ideas that (1) the body holds data and (2) we can tap into that data and influence our behavior by accessing proper areas of the brain or the body.

Work with implicit memory can take many forms, as the table in Appendix A demonstrates. However, for the purposes of this book, we will keep our focus on three types of brain-based therapy practiced at my center: EMDR,

Brainspotting, and Neurofeedback—in part because these are the three modalities I am trained in and currently practice.

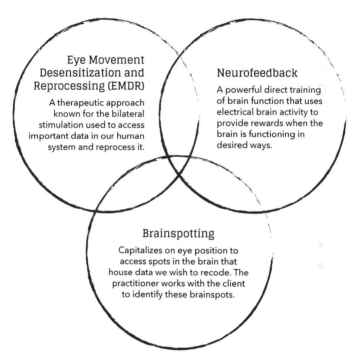

Three Highlighted Brain-Based Approaches
(Excellent for Changing Implicit Memory)

Eye Movement Desensitization and Reprocessing (EMDR)

A therapeutic approach known for the bilateral stimulation used to access important data in our human system and reprocess it.

Neurofeedback

A powerful direct training of brain function that uses electrical brain activity to provide rewards when the brain is functioning in desired ways.

Brainspotting

Capitalizes on eye position to access spots in the brain that house data we wish to recode. The practitioner works with the client to identify these brainspots.

EMDR (EYE MOVEMENT DESENSITIZATION AND REPROCESSING)

This practice uses bilateral stimulation of both sides of the brain through eye movements, sounds, or tactile sensations. EMDR can offer quick results, particularly when used to treat visceral, single-incident adult experiences. In essence, this novel approach to therapy is able to pinpoint mental saboteurs in your life, desensitize you to those saboteurs' effects, and help reprocess them. EMDR is effective with implicit memory because by using the body as the portal, this nonverbal approach has the ability to pinpoint data that is not encoded with words.

When Francine Shapiro, who developed EMDR, was getting ready to begin her dissertation, she began thinking about brain function and reducing the effects of stress on the body. In the process, she began to observe her own stress levels in a specific way. One day, while walking through a park, she noticed that her distress levels had gone down. Intrigued, first she asked herself what she had been doing over the previous time period. Then, she performed a critical analysis of everything going on in her body and realized that her eyes had been scanning back and forth as she was walking along a path.

From there, Shapiro began researching the effects of bilateral stimulation on the brain, including how rapid eye movement affected sleep cycles. She theorized that while thinking about an upsetting event, bilateral stimulation helped access something in her brain that ended up being restorative and regenerative. This concept then formed the basis for further research on how to access pockets of internal data in a more focused way.[4]

Her full therapeutic approach includes eight phases of treatment and ensures that the client experiences the full and effective internal and behavioral changes they desire. Many people mistakenly believe that EMDR is only about the bilateral stimulation. In reality, it is a full therapeutic framework for making substantive changes in how we function. It includes more than just desensitizing the difficult data stored in our system. It also includes all that is required to prepare our system to do that effectively by building rapport, trust, history taking, goal setting, as well as reprogramming our system to enjoy new, more adaptive beliefs and defaults in functioning on both a psychological and physical level. These reprocessed internal codes put us in the ideal position to meet our therapeutic goals and thrive in the ways that are most important to us.

BRAINSPOTTING

The Brainspotting therapeutic approach centers on the correlation between eye position and specific memories and experiences housed in the body. In essence, these "brain spots" are physical spots that hold an active memory (explicit and implicit) tied to an undesired symp-

4   Francine Shapiro, *Eye Movement Desensitization and Reprocessing: Basic Principles, Protocols, and Procedures* (New York: Guildford Press, 1995).

tom or corresponding to the neural pathway you want to modify. Brainspotting helps to identify those spots, rework the way those pathways are laid out, and integrate them more adaptively into current-day behavior and functioning.

Founder David Grand was able to make astonishing gains while working with a young figure skater. While trying to access the mental block that had been sabotaging her attempts to land a triple toe loop, Grand noticed an eye wobble whenever her gaze moved past a certain point. By requesting that she maintain her gaze where he noticed the eye wobble, they uncovered a great deal of previously unknown information that her body was storing. It turns out that that very information was seemingly getting in the way of her performance on the ice because, the next day, she was finally able to land the triple toe loop that had been eluding her.

Encouraged by these results, Grand then began to research what could be accounting for her significant progress in treatment. By fine-tuning his approaches, he was able to consistently replicate results in areas that had previously been inaccessible. Grand named this new therapy "Brainspotting" for the way it accessed the correlating areas of the brain through eye position.[5]

---

5   David Grand, *Brainspotting: The Revolutionary New Therapy for Rapid and Effective Change* (Louisville, CO: Sounds True, 2013).

NEUROFEEDBACK

Neurofeedback is based on the understanding that brain waves can be modified the same way that brain chemistry can be modified to realize any number of physical, psychological, and emotional gains. Neurofeedback provides specific brain wave conditioning correlating with the different functions performed by different parts of the brain's anatomy.

With the aid of an electroencephalogram (EEG), brain function (including functionality impacted by implicit memory) can be changed through electrical reconditioning. Brain waves can be modified on an electrical level and conditioned or adjusted to go up or down to optimize functioning.[6]

For example, an individual may be operating in the world with very high delta brain waves. These high delta waves will largely remain in the same state throughout the day, making the person slow to process data, as if they just woke up. They're groggy, their minds are moving slower, and they find it hard to multitask. It's like having that feeling of disorientation—that "Where am I?" or "What am I doing?" kind of feeling—but all the time.

The good news, however, is that those delta brain waves

---

6   Jim Robbins, *A Symphony in the Brain: The Evolution of the New Brain Wave Biofeedback* (Grand Haven, MI: Audible Studios on Brilliance, 2008).

can be reconditioned to rest at a lower frequency, improving the brain's capacity to shift from one task to another or to take in new data. Neurofeedback achieves this by using an electrical reading of the brain waves and providing feedback through visual, auditory, and sensory stimuli that reward the brain when it is moving in the right direction. To use a basic analogy, it's much like training a dog. A dog doesn't know whether what it's doing is good or bad. However, the more it's rewarded for a certain behavior, the more it forges a positive association with that behavior in its brain.

THE BENEFITS OF BRAIN- OR BODY-BASED THERAPY

Traditional talk-based psychological therapies work similarly to brain- or body-based therapy in terms of goals and process. Often, these approaches can be highly effective. However, in other instances, they're limited by the linear, analytical, and verbal nature of the therapeutic interaction that functions primarily with conscious thoughts and explicit memories.

For instance, while traditional talk therapy can be effective for struggles with anxiety, helping the client to make new connections in the intellectual part of the brain, the process of deeper change can be time-consuming. Similarly, these insight-oriented therapies can and do use associations to bring up experiences held in the unconscious (which may therefore be tied to implicit memory). But often, the insights these therapies generate fail to support more visceral physiological changes in the body, which makes it more difficult to implement behavioral change. For example, a client may learn that his difficulties with intimacy stem from his challenging childhood upbringing. While this is a valuable insight, the physical distress experienced as attachments start to form, such as a racing heart or mind, do not subside with the insight alone. Talk-based therapy risks overlooking issues related to sensory memories (smell, sound, touch, etc.), as well as implicit memories that may be preverbal and preconscious.[7]

For clients like this, the kinds of nonverbal approaches offered by brain- or body-based therapy are a game-changer, providing invaluable tools for reprogramming and recontextualizing all the negative messages in the clients' unconscious minds without the need to consciously access them.

For many people, giving up conscious control often feels counterintuitive. They're not used to seeing results unless they're actively participating in the process. Often, during their first session of advanced brain-based work, I will hear clients say something like "I don't think I'm getting this right. My mind is wandering, I'm really foggy,

7   Bessel van der Kolk, *The Body Keeps the Score* (New York: Penguin Books, 2015).

and I'm seeing this obscure image that's not related to my problem at all." As more images continue to pop up in their mind, I explain that what they think is a "wandering mind" is actually an *engaged* mind—one that's actively accessing and reprocessing data as we speak.

This is the amazing power of the human system. Its ability to set up codes and help us adapt to new situations is remarkable. However, sometimes those adaptations outlive their usefulness: what may have made you adaptive in one moment may interfere with your ability to perform later in life.

My goal with this book is to show you that you can target and reprogram those now sabotaging adaptations. We all experience challenges in our lives, whether at work, in our personal relationships, in athletics, or in the pursuit of personal goals. However, by accessing your implicit memories, you can change your possibilities. Yes, this book is about overcoming roadblocks. But more importantly, it's about creating a shift in internal messaging to help you perform better in the here and now.

CHAPTER ONE

YOUR BIG,
BEAUTIFUL BRAIN

In a human, there are more than 125 trillion synapses just in the cerebral cortex alone. That's roughly equal to the number of stars in 1,500 Milky Way galaxies.

—STEPHEN SMITH, PHD

The brain is infinitely complex. It's more powerful than a million computers and creates an endless web of message centers that make us do what we do.[1] So much of the brain's activity is automatic and preprogrammed that we don't even notice it.

All parts of the brain work together to form a control panel that tells our bodies what to do, with or without our per-

---

1   T. Bartol, "Nanoconnectomic Upper Bound on the Variability of Synaptic Plasticity," *eLife* (2015), doi: 10.7554/eLife.10778.

mission. Say you want to get a drink of water. You have the thought, "Oh, I need some water," and certain parts of your brain engage, utilizing brain synapses to transmit information between your neurons that lead you to move your hand, grab a glass, and lift the glass to your mouth. Meanwhile, you're still breathing, and your heart is still pumping—functions you don't have to think about at all. In fact, after you've gotten yourself a glass of water many times, you don't have to think about that much, either, because the process gets stored in your procedural memory, one component of your implicit memory (see Chapter 2). It's amazing.

THE ANATOMY OF PSYCHOLOGY

Basic Brain Anatomy

Frontal and Prefrontal Cortex

Left Hemisphere
Controls the right side of the body (logical thought)

Right Hemisphere
Controls the left side of the body (creative/artistic)

Brain Stem
Controls basic bodily functions

Limbic System
Located in the center of the brain under the outer layer (Includes the hippocampus)

The brain is an incredible organ, with more complexity and functionality than we can possibly cover in this book. Here, we're focused on psychological health and how it informs various body states, so we'll concentrate on the parts of the brain that have the most impact on mental well-being: how we relate to others, how we feel, and how we adapt to challenging situations. Several parts of the brain are involved, including the prefrontal cortex, the frontal cortex, and the brain stem.

PREFRONTAL CORTEX

The prefrontal cortex, located in the forebrain, is the seat of executive functioning, high-level decision-making, and social interaction. This is where we form conscious habits, such as saying "Please" and "Thank you." It's also where we make the decisions that create our personalities and affect the way we relate to others. Not surprisingly, the biggest changes in the prefrontal cortex happen during the developmental years, up to age twenty-five.[2]

The prefrontal cortex is often the target of psychological therapies because this is where we learn to relate to others, negotiate conflict, and manage intimacy. The prefrontal cortex processes lessons about how safe the world is, how to approach goal-setting, and how to react

2   S.V. Siddiqui et al., "Neuropsychology of Prefrontal Cortex," *Indian Journal of Psychiatry* 50, no. 3 (July 2008), 202–8.

to punishment and reward. It's a major player in risk tolerance, adaptability, and flexibility.

FRONTAL CORTEX

The frontal cortex is also in the forebrain and affects thought. Picture it as the headquarters of communication and personality, which inform emotional expression, problem-solving, memory, sexual behavior, language, and judgment. The frontal cortex holds the networks that create and maintain patterns of behavior, such as language. Like the prefrontal cortex, the frontal cortex is most flexible and malleable during the developmental years.

When people learn a language, including grammar and preferred ways to communicate in their cultural communities, there's a lot of activity in the frontal cortex. Interestingly, people who learn more than one language can expand their frontal-cortex capacity because the brain is being challenged to make multiple connections between sounds and meaning.[3] To increase any type of brain capacity, people must engage in challenges that keep their brains growing through increased firing of the synapses.

---

3   T.H. Bak et al., "Never Too Late? An Advantage on Tests of Auditory Attention Extends to Late Bilinguals," *Frontiers in Psychology* 5 (2014): 485.

BRAIN STEM

The brain stem controls basic body functions. Connected to the spinal cord, the brain stem drives information flow between the brain and the rest of the body. When someone is in a coma but is still able to breathe without life support, this is largely due to the work of the brain stem. Its job is to protect and maintain the core functions of the body: breathing, heartbeat, and blood flow.

The brain stem is particularly important to the study of how emotions relate to bodily function.[4] Take fear, for instance. When someone is worried about presenting a pitch to their company's board of directors, what happens to their body? Their throat may close up, their heart may start beating faster, and they may sweat, even possibly starting to panic. If we can affect the brain stem, we can short-circuit the physical reaction and lower the person's perceived stress. In my work, I've seen people change their physical and cognitive reactions to situations that previously overwhelmed them—all by accessing their hidden control panel and reworking their implicit memory networks.

Can you imagine, right now, finally overcoming that fear of public speaking? Can you imagine being able to finally set aside your preoccupation with gaining weight or being undermined in a board meeting? By understanding more

4   Peter Levine, *Waking the Tiger: Healing Trauma* (Berkeley: North Atlantic Books, 1997).

fully the power of implicit memory and how to change the codes stored there, we find that these types of outcomes are truly possible.

The Central Nervous System

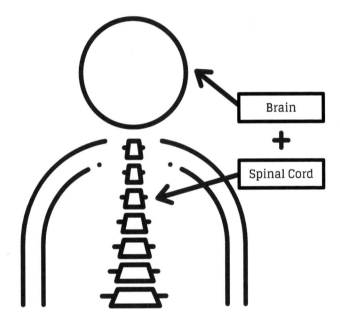

Connecting everything are neural pathways. These pathways connect different parts of the brain, as well as the brain to the rest of the nervous system (the brain + spinal cord = central nervous system [CNS]). Neural pathways are the bundles of nerves you may have heard described as "white matter."

Neural pathways transmit the messages that govern our responses. How do we experience excitement about our favorite football team winning the Super Bowl, for instance? We feel happy because of the endorphins transmitted through our neural pathways.

Our system is always scanning for the best way to respond at any given time. The pathways that are established as a result are not always optimal in the long run, but they become the default responses nonetheless. By taking the established neural pathway time and time again, we reinforce it, even if the adaptation wears out its welcome.[5] Those well-worn patterns can then hold us back, even though they were initially adaptive to a different set of circumstances (which we'll talk more about in the following chapters).

NEURAL NETWORKS

Neural networks are created when connections form between neural pathways. These connections are initially adaptive, based on the resources that were available to the person during the time of a given experience. Later, as circumstances change, those pathways can outgrow

---

5   J. Hain, "The Neuroscience of Behavior Change: Helping Patients Change Behaviors by Understanding the Brain," *Health Transformers* (2017), https://healthtransformer.co/ the-neuroscience-of-behavior-change-bcb567fa83c1.

their usefulness. Neural networks connect everything, and when they start pairing up, they become intertwined.

Say you witness a plane crash. Your neural network links the concepts of planes and disaster together, and now you cannot go into the airport without experiencing extreme stress. Neural networks like these become deeply ingrained shortcuts. The shortcut was put in placc to protect you since the code "plane = disaster" was established in your implicit memory system. But now you miss out on some great experiences because a part of your brain no longer codes planes as safe, and so taking the longer way around is incentivized in your system.

Luckily, these trails can be rerouted—not consciously, but by changing the mapping in the implicit memories stored in your brain.[6] When brain mapping changes, behavioral change becomes much more attainable. As a simple example, consider a student who is afraid to raise his hand in class. He sees that other people do it all the time, and they're fine. They're fine even if they make a mistake or have the wrong answer. He knows this intellectually, but when he tries it himself, anxiety takes over. Now imagine the same student on the first try feeling comfortable and confident, as if his reaction set point

6   K. Cherry, "What Is Brain Plasticity? How Experience Changes the Brain," *Very Well Mind* (2018), https://www.verywellmind.com/what-is-brain-plasticity-2794886.

had been reprogrammed. After this reprogramming, he would have no trouble expressing himself in class.

We too can make changes like this by capitalizing on the way neural networks operate.

ADAPTIVE MEMORY NETWORKS

Adaptive memory networks are networks in our brain that continue to be effective at supporting optimal behavior in the present. These networks allow us to hold a moment of distress both in our mind's eye and deep within our system in a complete and balanced way. Back when humankind faced constant threats to its survival—think lions, tigers, and bears—people had to be vigilant, constantly scan for danger, and keep their bodies in tune to survive. In order to balance all of this successfully, their adaptive memory networks had to keep reminding them of their strength and abilities to outrun or outperform their predators.

Biologically speaking, our adaptive networks have served a useful purpose. However, in the present day, when we're no longer concerned with outrunning or outperforming lions, tigers, and bears, this very same network could be getting in the way. An adaptive memory network is balanced in our overall understanding of our value, ability, survivorship, and so on. If, for some reason, what we used to adapt to a prior circumstance is no longer serving us in the present day, then we can find these very same coping strategies to have become maladaptive. They can in turn become a factor that sabotages our present-day desires without us even realizing it.

Luckily, once we understand the way this process can work in our own implicit memory system, we become more empowered and self-compassionate. We understand the need to invest in more sophisticated measures to truly change what no longer serves us (see Appendix A). I have seen clients who, without this knowledge, have stumbled around suffering for years with misinformation prior to our work together. Understanding that any neural network can be reverse-engineered to our benefit is powerful. In the reprogramming work of advanced brain-based therapies, we can actually access these negative messages hidden in our implicit memory and use our adaptive networks to change them in positive ways.

BRAIN HEMISPHERES

Brain-based therapies such as EMDR and Brainspotting use bilateral stimulation to process and integrate implicit memories. In general, the right side of the brain controls the left side of the body and vice versa. The right side of the brain is associated with creativity and artistry, spatial ability, and facial recognition. The left side of the brain is associated with math, science, and logic. Processing images and information across both hemispheres is a powerful way to loosen and rework data stored in neural pathways. Throughout this book, we'll witness how brain-based therapies take advantage of bilateral processing.

LIMBIC SYSTEM

The limbic system is an important system that is focused on survival. The system is commonly referred to as the fight, flight, or freeze mechanism—the automatic instinct that tells you what to do when you're in danger. When we need to run fast to escape a burning building, the limbic system makes sure that happens. When signals go awry, though, and we start reacting to neutral—or even positive—stimuli with fear, the results can present unnecessary challenges in our lives. Because the limbic reaction is automatic in design in order to harness the instantaneous reaction required to survive danger, it can resist change. Fortunately, some of the newer therapeutic approaches and case studies illustrated in this book will illustrate how even the most dire of coding, the coding that originates in our core drive to survive, can be changed.[7]

---

7   Peter Levine, *In an Unspoken Voice: How the Body Releases Trauma and Restores Goodness* (Berkeley: North Atlantic Books, 2010).

MAPPING THE BRAIN

A cautionary note on the limits of brain mapping: it's tempting to think that the anatomy of the brain has a one-to-one connection with the mind and the body. With the latest medical technology, we can see what's going on in the brain. We've all seen impressive images from functional MRIs that illustrate different types of brain activity. Perceiving that activity, however, doesn't necessarily tell us what's going on for a person physically or emotionally. To date, few significant scientific studies exist on the effects of psychological mapping on neurology, and the scientific community has been unable to draw concrete conclusions. For now, we know just enough to know there's so much more to learn.

NEUROPLASTICITY: THE KEY TO CHANGE

The reason brain- or body-based therapies are so effective is that the brain is plastic. It does change in structure and function in response to experience.[8] Humans are built to learn. That's why practicing a new skill over and over can change our automatic behaviors even though it's often a struggle to do so. Learning through repetition can be a laborious process at best. At worst, it can seem impossible to reset all the learning that came before.

When we work with implicit memory using brain- or body-based therapies, we can make changes more easily, quickly, and effectively than we can through conscious effort. Take, for example, a roommate who simply

---

8   Daniel Siegel, *Mind: A Journey to the Heart of Being Human* (New York & London: W.W. Norton & Company, 2017).

cannot keep his space organized. He wants to be neat and respectful, and he tries. He reads books and takes classes to develop his organizing skills. Still, every room he uses ends up a mess, and he doesn't know how to stop.

The messy roommate may have some encoded associations getting in the way of changing his behavior. Perhaps when he was young, his volatile father came in to his clean room and beat him, so now the young man feels safer with clutter all around. The code of "clean = heartache/pain" is in his implicit memory. His neurons learned to fire together, creating this code in search of safety, and then they wired together making that shortcut the one that plays over and over in the desire to avoid being hurt again. This happens whether he remembers the incidents or not.

Brain-based therapies can change his behavior by getting him to stop taking the shortcut his brain created long ago. When we shift the neural pathway, we change the messages that lead to the unconscious thought "Don't clean up your room." With tools like EMDR, Brainspotting, and Neurofeedback, we can access and open pathways he doesn't have conscious access to. Shifting the neural pathways removes resistance and makes change much more accessible.

THE BRAIN IS MADE TO CHANGE

In this chapter, we've touched on several of the brain's amazing functions. The things the brain can do, via the central nervous system, and the messages our bodies receive are nothing short of amazing. How those things happen is astoundingly complex. On one hand, we survive because of the automatic reactions stored in our brains and bodies. (How many times have you heard a story about someone in a car crash who simply lifted the car up off his fellow victim with a strength he never had before?) On the other hand, some of those stored memories hold us back.

Fortunately, the brain is not made only to store information; it is made to evolve. We can harness that plasticity to achieve incredible results. People who want to run a race faster, get a promotion at work, or improve a relationship can use the brain's strengths to do so. This book is about becoming the architect of your own life. You can control your responses by changing things in your system you may not even be aware of. You can remove things that no longer serve you and replace them with what you really want. We've always known humans have a remarkable ability to change and adapt: now we have technologies that can help the brain make necessary shifts and incorporate them into the body.

WHY THIS MATTERS

Many adult adoptees remain unaware that their time in an orphanage or other sensory data they took in before the age of three may be impacting them now. They have never heard of concepts like implicit memory or neuroplasticity, and so they mistakenly conclude they are broken or intrinsically flawed simply because they struggle with relationships/attachments or mental health issues. The dominant narrative around adoption is that it's an ideal "solution" where children should only feel grateful and blessed to have received a better fate. While this may be factually true in some circumstances, it overlooks the fact that, for an infant, the act of relinquishment includes the loss of the mother. This loss includes sights, smells, and sounds that become irreplaceable and, therefore, can be felt as a significant loss to the infant.

As an adoptee myself, this hit home for me when I had my first child. I worked so hard in those early months to further my bond with my daughter through our skin-on-skin contact, as recommended by all of the medical professionals who were working with me. During those early months of sleepless nights, my focus was on providing constant care to my child and nurturing the incredible bond that we shared (and were continuing to build).

At some point in those first six months of my daughter's life, my own mother sent me some of my baby clothes and pictures from my own early moments. The earliest photograph of me was one I had seen many times in a photo album as I was growing up. This time, since the photo was sent in an envelope, I was able to see its backside, which included a date—over two months after my birth—and an inscription: "The day we picked Julie up." I had always known about my adoption but never had the reality of my early life hit me so hard. I literally fell into a nearby chair at that moment. Being told I was "adopted as a baby" was one thing. Understanding that, for over two months, I was living with many other unclaimed babies in an orphanage was quite another, especially with the juxtaposition of what was unfolding in my own child's early life.

This lack of knowledge adoptees experience can lead to years of misdiagnosis for those adoptees struggling with mental health issues. If no trauma is recognized in the time period before adoption, then the understanding of existing symptoms related to attachment trauma will be missed and pathologized.

As an adoptee myself, this struggle matters to me. Their struggle is my own.

My journey to master working in nonverbal approaches stems from a deep desire to find tools that can address injuries housed in the body—both in my own and those of my patients—that have no words or memories attached to them. In that way, finding so many ways to address preverbal and preconscious distress in our bodies is personal.

It pains me to come into contact with so many adult adoptees who have spent years in therapy with no abatement of their symptoms and no relief in sight. It pains me even further to meet so many mental health professionals with no training on how to work within the adoption triad (adoptive parents + birth parents + adopted person = adoption triad). The resolutions and relief I have seen as a direct result of more sophisticated understanding and compassion about the adoptee experience on the part of the general public, mental health practitioners, and adoptees alike has been incredible. It continues to inspire my own work to empower through understanding and working with implicit memory.

CHAPTER TWO

THE IMPLICIT MEMORY REVOLUTION

Neurons that fire together, wire together.

—DONALD HEBB

Implicit memory can be demonstrated with an analogy of fabric and weaving: the pattern on top is the conscious memory, while the underlying weave makes up your implicit memory. Someone can make colors and patterns, but the underlying structure remains hard to see. In this tapestry, each thread making up each pattern is connected. If you pull just one thread, it affects the entire pattern. However, thanks to the implicit memory revolution, we are learning how to identify and target specific threads—threads we don't have conscious access to—and reprogram them. In other words, all those neurons that have been firing together can be reprogrammed to fire apart.

How can we do this? In the simplest terms, our brains have plasticity. They can change. By accessing what is coded in our implicit memory system, we can modify and adapt the underlying core beliefs or core messages that govern our survival and operation. These implicit beliefs are encoded in the brain through sensory data that are neither intellectual nor conscious. Most of these data are visceral and sensory in nature, such as my visual memory of the fire exploding all over my kitchen or the sound of that event. As a result, accessing this data is often a matter of identifying the bodily sensations that correspond with a particular roadblock. By accessing the corresponding sensation, our systems then become open to processing out the no-longer-helpful implicit memory and coding, and in turn, more open to reworking the code to be adaptive for the present day.

3 Types of Implicit Memory

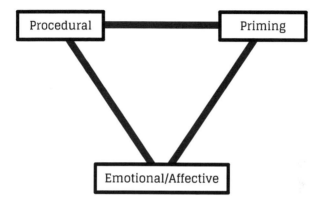

Implicit memory includes millions of messages moving through the brain that are sensory in nature. They include both preverbal and preconscious information, as well as visceral data about how the world works and how to be adaptive in it. Not only is our life informed by this constant flow of seemingly invisible data traveling in our human system, but also outside of our consciousness, we are continually absorbing new information. Using neurons, synapses, and neural pathways, messages can be carried back and forth between the body (through the spine) and the brain. Each of those inputs, whether it's the sensation of breathing deeply, smelling the mildew-laden leaves, or experiencing steak and cheese, sends messages to the brain and subsequently to the body. The conscious part of the brain has little awareness of some of these sensory messages, which ultimately become stored in our system as implicit memory.

PROCEDURAL MEMORY

There are three different types of implicit memory. Of these, procedural memory is the most commonly known. Procedural memories often involve specific repetitive motions, such as picking up a glass of water or riding a bike. Consider for a moment all the different steps to riding a bike. You have a million different things to think about: learning to balance, how to use the pedals and brakes, and how to pay attention to your surroundings. Then, you have to figure out how to put all your knowledge and muscle memory together at once. How can anyone possibly do all of those things at the same time?

At first, we can't. There's so much data involved, and coordination between functions required, that the process can be somewhat overwhelming. However, if you're a bike rider, as I am, you probably haven't thought about any of that in a long time. Instead, you just do it. By now, your human system's knowledge of how to ride a bike has become part of your procedural memory. The process is so integrated into your mind and body that it no longer requires conscious thought. You just get on your bike and start riding, leaving your conscious mind free to think of other totally different things.

When I'm out for a ride, I might be thinking about priorities in my life, my interpersonal relationships, or any social plans I may have coming up. I'm not thinking about biking because it's completely routine. I might even be talking politics or community happenings while riding along with a friend. I'm not thinking about riding the bike, yet I'm doing it the whole time. Stored procedural memory is in the unconscious. This knowledge is available to you, but most of us consciously access it only if a difficult situation arises. Otherwise, we don't give it much thought.

PRIMING

While procedural memory is one aspect of implicit memory, other types of implicit memory run much deeper than that. In fact, some aspects of the data stored in our implicit memory are formed before we even have conscious thoughts or memories. The second type of implicit memory is called "priming." Put simply, with priming, exposure to one stimulus influences a person's response to a second stimulus. These stimuli can be perceptual, conceptual, or semantic. With priming, the person is unaware of any guiding influence because that influence is operating in the unconscious. The power of priming is often exploited in sophisticated marketing and advertising campaigns, enabling companies to deeply influence spending habits.

One interesting study highlights the power of priming. In a wine store, researchers chose alternate days to play German or French music over the sound system. This was the first stimulus (an auditory one). By doing so, the researchers found a statistically significant correlation between the country of origin of the wine consumers bought and the country of origin of the music playing throughout the store. In other words, when they played French music, the customers were much more likely to buy French wine, and the same was true for German wine and music. The consumers, of course, remained unaware of this priming influence on their purchase, but the evidence was overwhelming.[1]

EMOTIONAL/AFFECTIVE MEMORY

The third type of implicit memory—and the one we will spend the most time discussing in this book—is known as "emotional" or "affective memory." Simply put, the human brain is infinitely more complex than any computer humankind has ever built. It is constantly scanning, taking in new data, and seeing whether that information matches what's already stored—which is why it is sometimes hard to change old habits. Often, your system will reject new information in favor of the knowledge it already has. It's as if it's saying, "No. Doesn't compute.

1   A.C. North, D.J. Hargreaves, and J. McKendrick, "The influence of in-store music on wine selections," *Journal of Applied Psychology* 84, no. 2. (1999): 271–76.

Doesn't match. Throw that out!" When it encounters a new experience, however, it's eager to store that, taking in data on every sensory level.

Emotional/affective memory is the memory connecting sensation to an overall state of mind (e.g., "plane crash = death" or "clean room = danger"). Remember that the codes are not created in a verbal or linear format. Rather, emotional/affective implicit memory might hold the sensory information of the sound of the announcements of the airport, the feel of the shuffling experience of the plane's boarding process, the sensation of the layout of the plane as cues to evoke a felt sense of dread, an increased heart rate, difficulty breathing, and a desire to run.

Significant theorists in prenatal and developmental psychology, such as Freud, Erickson, Piaget, and Mahler, believe this process begins the moment our human systems come online. Even inside the womb, our growing bodies begin taking in information (though none of us explicitly remembers these earliest moments of our lives).[2] At birth, the process only accelerates. Infants take in a ton of data about their environment and relationships, most of which becomes foundational elements in their network of implicit memories.[3]

---

2   J. Hopson, "Fetal Psychology," *Psychology Today*, September 1998.

3   P. Ogden and J. Fisher, *Sensorimotor Psychotherapy: Interventions for Trauma and Attachment* (New York and London: W.W. Norton & Company, 2015).

While our systems store countless memories in our unconscious right from the very beginning, conscious memory usually doesn't begin until around four or five, though sometimes as early as three. For this reason, effective techniques around comforting a newborn often involve replicating the environment of the womb through swaddling and containment. Since infants and toddlers don't yet have a sense of themselves explicitly, they rely heavily on familiar sensory cues from the environment in order to establish a sense of security and well-being.[4] Should those cues be missing from their early environment, the infant will employ survival coping mechanisms. These adaptations could then become future roadblocks stored in implicit memory for the reasons outlined below.

Acclaimed psychiatrist Dan Siegel identified four conditions that influence when emotional or affective data will become stored in our implicit memory as opposed to explicit memory. All are related to the functioning (or lack of functioning) of the hippocampus, a part of the brain, since the hippocampus is required to move data into explicit memory. The hippocampus processes sensory data into a coherent picture and gives it a time stamp to allow it to be filed into a conscious memory in our explicit memory system.

---

4   Gabor Maté, *In the Realm of Hungry Ghosts: Close Encounters with Addiction* (Berkeley: North Atlantic Books, 2008).

1. Before thirty-six months of age, when the hippocampus is not yet typically fully functioning. For this reason, it is called the preverbal and preconscious time period.
2. If the hippocampus becomes damaged due to trauma. A biological injury or brain injury can cause the hippocampus not to function.
3. If the system is overwhelmed and dissociation has occurred. Dissociation is when our system is not conscious to what is occurring.
4. If cortisol levels get too high due to stress, the hippocampus can be temporarily turned off. This occurs in the case of situational trauma or distress.[5]

THE POWER OF IMPLICIT MEMORY

Implicit memories can have a powerful effect on how we live our lives, even though we often don't understand them or are even unaware of them.

For instance, perhaps you've never liked the color yellow. You're not sure why, and you probably haven't even given it much thought, but something about it disagrees with you. Then one day, you learn that you survived a fire when you were little, and your parents carried you out in a yellow blanket. In your unconscious mind, the distress-

---

5   Daniel J. Siegel, "Domains of Integration," July 27, 2010, MP3 audio, http://www.drdansiegel. com/uploads/DomainsofIntegration.mp3.

ing element of that experience was forever associated
with the color yellow.

While it would be nice to know the implicit roots of all
our opinions and behaviors, the truth is that we rarely get
the data to make these kinds of connections. The benefit
of brain- or body-based therapies, however, is that you
don't have to have all the explicit data to target an implicit
reaction that has outgrown its usefulness and change it.

As a result, as in our example, you may end up hating the
color yellow for no known reason. It evokes something in
you, and you find it nauseating. For the most part, you've
been able to get by in life even with your strong negative reaction to yellow, but what happens when you're
hired for an exciting new job and the entire interior of the
office is yellow? On a logical level, you love your job. However, every time you enter the office, you feel a sense of
repulsion that is sometimes so strong that you've begun
looking for excuses to meet with clients somewhere else.

Brain- or body-based therapy can change inputs to your
visceral experience. By accessing problematic visceral
data, like feeling nauseated when seeing the color yellow,
the advanced brain- or body-based therapist can begin
processing the data of that experience until it is no longer
distressing. Then the therapist can create a new, positive association with the yellow blanket or even the color

yellow from the client's own already-stored memories. This new association of safety with yellow can now be encoded as a new neural pathway to follow as the color yellow is introduced in the present day.

When I work with a client, we start with the symptoms the client wants to change. If they can identify the root cause of their symptoms, that data can be helpful, but it's not essential. The power of working with implicit memories through nonverbal therapeutic practices is that you don't have to know the story that gave rise to them to modify the coding in your system. For those who don't have access to the stories of their distressing experiences—perhaps they grew up in foster care or didn't have a family historian—such therapeutic processes are invaluable. These can allow them to heal from that experience without ever having to consciously know exactly what happened. Maybe even more importantly, they don't have to relive those horrible moments in order to heal from them.

Following full therapeutic processing, clients often report immediate results. Returning to the example above, if you were disturbed by the color yellow, processing the implicit memory tied to yellow would soon allow you to walk into the office painted yellow ready to take on the world. No more scheduling off-site meetings with clients; the once-nauseating office environment is suddenly fine. Your neural network will have been reprogrammed to associate yellow with other more positive responses already in your adaptive memory network.

If you are an older person, you may not have access to the story of your aversion to yellow. Your parents may have passed on, and no one else may be around to provide the data of the yellow blanket and the fire. This difficult implicit memory may have stuck with you for decades, but you don't need to know the details of it to change the neural pathway. Nor do you need to relive the memory of the fire to understand why yellow nauseates you, which is more of an intellectual pursuit. All you need to know is that somewhere in your brain, a negative association has been encoded around the color yellow, but with the new processing tactics, you don't need to relive that negative experience to rework your connection. You can change your relationship to yellow by targeting the color itself.

This is the power of the human brain and body. Your system holds data whether you consciously know it or not. And by harnessing the power of your implicit memory, you will be able to access that data and optimize it for the benefit of your life.

IMPLICIT MEMORY CAN IMPACT GENERATIONS

We often think of the process of seeking answers and resolution as a linear concept with a logical flow, much like reading a historical review of our lives in a textbook. However, as author and internationally recognized trauma expert Bessel van der Kolk explains in *The Body Keeps the Score*, the brain doesn't work that way.[6] The brain already has all the mapping you need to arrive at the answers you seek. The challenge for many of us is learning how to get to that answer and initiate the processes that will bring resolution.

This understanding serves as the basis for much of our work at the Viva Center. While our clients are often disappointed to learn that we don't practice memory recovery, we explain that concrete memory is not necessary for effective processing. In many senses, memory recovery is more of a research project than the type of change practice we are deeply invested in at my center.

As such, a big part of our job involves resetting clients' expectations. For instance, many of our clients who are adult adoptees think that once they meet their birth parents, they will no longer feel anxious or depressed, and therefore believe that everything will be better for them. While I wish this were the case, unfortunately, our minds don't work that way. Connecting with one's biological parents does not change the mapping in a person's body or undo any distressing loss stemming from

6   Bessel van der Kolk, *The Body Keeps the Score* (New York: Penguin Books, 2014).

relinquishment.[7] Similarly, the knowledge that I survived that kitchen fire didn't eliminate the symptoms I had around my illogical belief that I was going to die (illogical because I had already survived). Rerouting your neural pathways cannot be accomplished through analytical or practical change.

If analysis were all it took to mitigate harmful implicit processes, then treating someone with a destructive behavior such as anorexia, for example, would be much simpler. All one would need to do is show the client that they are not overweight, perhaps through images and data that demonstrates their body mass index to be in the appropriate range. As any practitioner knows, however, such a conversation is not enough for a person with anorexia to begin developing healthier eating habits.[8] Without facts and logic, oftentimes we can feel out of control or uncertain how to move forward. However, in both those cases where facts and logic are unavailable and those where they are insufficient to change behavior, brain-based therapies offer a game-changing alternative.

I've worked with clients raised in poverty, for instance, who constantly received the message throughout their

---

7   Nancy Verrier, *The Primal Wound: Understanding the Adopted Child* (California: Verrier Publishing, 1993).

8   Bessel van der Kolk, "How Trauma Lodges in the Body," *On Being*, March 9, 2017, podcast, https://onbeing.org/programs/ bessel-van-der-kolk-how-trauma-lodges-in-the-body-mar2017/.

early lives that there weren't enough resources and that they had to be careful, or they wouldn't survive. This sustained messaging implicitly encoded itself into their neural pathways, resulting in a lifelong drive to accumulate wealth. However, because their core money belief is one of scarcity, they may not invest logically or to the best of their abilities because they feel compelled to hold on to every dollar. I've witnessed similar implicit adaptations having occurred in clients who grew up in households without food. Because of that sensory experience of not having enough, these clients unwittingly starve themselves out of a misplaced desire to conserve what they have.

Other clients have come to us with the deeply ingrained experience of having grown up with either a sick sibling or one who passed away. Often, these surviving siblings have adapted by learning to be helpful, to not be too loud, and to not ask for much. Through these adaptations, their brains became encoded to believe that being in loving relationships means being invisible and not putting too many demands on the system. As they moved into adulthood, these clients became withholding of their own needs, desires, or anything else that would connect someone to them.

Another client of mine experienced his brother's death when they were young, which affected many of his behaviors as he grew into adulthood. There are countless neural pathways that support the feelings of energy and excitement that comes with letting someone into your life. Unfortunately, as he grew up adapting to the loss of his brother and his parents' resulting depression, these pathways didn't form as strongly in his mind. Rather, he grew up unconsciously apprehensive of connecting with other people. His implicit memory system had associated closeness and attachment with hurt. It took him years to understand the levels to which these sensory inputs impacted his development. So entrenched were these neural pathways that a logical, storytelling-based approach would not have been enough to address his core issues.

Even if we understand our story and are able to logically recite it, we may find that we have a difficult time changing the protective emotional conclusions that go along with it. Often, this stems from a distressing experience relating to our own emotional needs that was never fully resolved. As renowned addiction expert Gabor Mate notes, "The subtle, virtually undetectable nature of implicit memory is one reason it can have powerful effects on our mental lives."[9]

In this client's experience, whenever he would get close

9   Gabor Mate, *In the Realm of Hungry Ghosts: Close Encounters with Addiction* (California: North Atlantic Books, 2010).

to someone, his body would start flashing warning signals that there was imminent loss or excruciating heartbreak ahead. He didn't consciously think that, but was rather responding to the sensations in his body. These new relationships were different from the one he had enjoyed with his brother, but the implicit memories of my client's experiences at the end of his brother's life nevertheless followed him through into each new experience. The story of loss had been encoded into the fabric of his neural networks, but through the use of Brainspotting, he was able to rework what that story meant to him and then separate it from his present-day attempts to feel connection on a deep level.

DIFFERENT APPROACHES TO IMPLICIT-MEMORY ACCESS

Humans have put forward different ideas and theories about how the brain works for thousands of years. During the past three decades, our quest to understand the brain has taken us to the study of the unconscious and the hidden access points of our minds. In broad terms, that's what neuropsychology is all about: understanding the ways in which psychological inputs and functions affect the brain and vice versa.

Aside from the three approaches highlighted throughout this book (EMDR, Brainspotting, and Neurofeedback), neuropsychology has validated a number of therapeutic approaches for accessing implicit memory that don't involve reprogramming or access through the brain, but rather through the body. For instance, powerful approaches like Peter Levine's Somatic Experiencing and Pat Ogden's Sensorimotor Psychotherapy both utilize the body as an entry point to discovering and reworking material stored in implicit memory. Either offers a method of accessing the way we hold this material in our human system. While methodologies such as these may vary in approach, they all have one thing in common: connecting the anatomical physiological human experience with the implicit psychological experiences and corresponding symptoms.

Ultimately, we are all different, and so the therapeutic approaches that work best for us may be a personal preference or a reflection of the uniqueness of our own experiences. Whatever approach you choose, be it the three brain-based therapies that are the focus of this book, or the many other body-based approaches listed in the resources section (Appendix A) at the end, my goal is for you to feel empowered by the options available to you. Everyone is different. The best way to approach and reprogram the obstacles being held in your implicit memory is the one that feels most comfortable to you.

NOT ALL DISTRESS IS EQUAL

Some of us have lived relatively stress-free lives and need to focus on reprogramming only a single incident or mild disappointment. Others have experienced a variety of distressing events that weave a much deeper and more complicated fabric of implicit memories in their unconscious.

Whatever the case, brain-based therapies can be highly effective. A clinician trained in these advanced practices can help pinpoint a client's therapeutic goal and, through direct application, help that client regain control.

Our systems clean house when we sleep. We regenerate everything. Wounds heal, and energy is restored. That's why rest is so important after surgery, an accident, or even a big accomplishment. Recovery is what our bodies are programmed to do, and psychological recovery is just as important as physical recovery. Just as nightmares help clean the mind of distressing content, so too does brain-based therapy by reprocessing implicit memories.

For those who have distressing experiences in their past, the ability to access them—even if that person doesn't recall or understand them—and reprogram a new response is a powerful tool. No longer do these experiences have to impact our relationships, our job performance, or our overall quality of life. Instead of feeling stuck on a plateau—or worse, stuck in survival mode—we can move forward with our lives. We can rewire our systems to thrive.

DIFFERENT PATHS TO NONVERBAL TREATMENT

Many of the people who seek out brain- or body-based therapies have endured significant hardship, such as near-deadly encounters, unspeakable violence, and family tragedies. Since they do have memories of their struggles, they remain perplexed as to why troublesome symptoms are lingering well after the hardship has passed. Typically, they have heard of these nonverbal therapeutic options through friends, professional recommendations, or their own research as effective approaches to mitigate overwhelming symptoms. Since our systems are built to survive, we have many neural networks that will form and adapt around the implicit memory of these experiences, not just what we know consciously. Remember, the limbic system (our fight-flight-or-freeze response to threat) impacts many other systems in our body. This is why the data encoded in our implicit memory cannot be reprogrammed intellectually.

Others seeking nonverbal treatment approaches are not aware that they even have data stored in implicit memory. Unaware of any traumas to process, their symptoms may be the result of experiences that are not accessible in conscious thought. Rather, they come in motivated to excel in a target area of their life, such as their professional life or their personal life, and they come seeking results. Often confused as to why their system is getting in their own way, they are receptive to learning about different ways to access their full lived experience, not just the explicit memories stored.

The following client stories demonstrate how much influence data stored in implicit memory can have on your present life, especially when you struggle with roadblocks to success. More importantly, these stories highlight how nonverbal approaches to connect with data stored in implicit memory can transform lives in order to thrive.

A PROFESSIONAL DILEMMA

A woman came to me through a referral from her primary therapist. She wanted some targeted, brain-based work. Why? Because her prestigious position required extensive travel—and although this client had flown regularly for many, many years, she could no longer physically get on a plane. The job she had worked incredibly hard to get was now in jeopardy.

A few months back, she had been on a flight for work when the pilot announced to the passengers to prepare for a crash landing. Everyone on the plane survived, but the tumultuous emergency landing left many of the passengers injured—whether mentally, physically, or both. My client had an especially rough time of it, suffering a significant back injury and blacking out before the plane ultimately landed and the emergency personnel began tending to the passengers.

Even when speaking with me in the safe confines of our office, the mere thought of boarding a plane and flying brought about low-level anxiety. In her mind, she would hear the various airport announcements and other standard noise, and her body would start reacting. Sometimes she would suffer full-blown panic attacks: her breathing would become erratic, she would break into a cold sweat, and eventually, she would be become unable to walk or talk.

This mental toll was only exacerbated by the demands of her job, which still required frequent travel. In an attempt to avoid planes, she'd take long trips by train and try to find other ways to avoid flying. Her anxiety was crippling her.

Like many of my clients, this client had already tried working her experiences out in other ways before coming to me. She had thought cognitive behavioral therapy would be useful, as it has proven effective in working with anxiety disorders, obsessive-compulsive thinking, and attention deficit disorders. However, such a methodology wasn't as effective in treating an overloaded limbic system that insisted she was going to die. By the time she came to work with me, she had tried a lot of strategies and had read a lot of self-help books, but none of it had worked. She was desperate.

I learned all of this during our initial sessions as I worked to build rapport with her, understand the scope of what was happening, and start planning where to target. I also learned that, aside from the plane crash, she had relatively few distressing experiences in her developmental history. She had a strong base from which to build, which would help speed up the process considerably.

The client and I used EMDR to help her process the crash. It took a few long sessions to peel back the underlying base messaging in her body, which, in this case, was a limbic system that had kicked in during the emergency landing and told her, "This is your death moment." In that moment, her limbic system was only doing its job—telling her when she was dying so she could disconnect and not feel the suffering of a tragic death. Now, that death message had become strongly associated with airplanes and airports. Her system was routinely doing everything it would do in a near-death situation to protect her, create a casing around her awareness, and prepare her for death.

Through EMDR, her system was able to (1) desensitize that death message and (2) take in the message that she had already identified as a goal of her therapy. The message that "planes = living" was the message she actually wanted to deliver to her brain. This second point is an essential component of EMDR protocol. During the initial intake sessions, we ask clients to consider logically what they would like to believe instead and what they wish they could tell the cells of their bodies—the fiber of their being—about what they've experienced. This helps focus the reprocessing effort and move clients toward their therapeutic goals. After only a few sessions, her anxiety related to flying was all but gone.

The anxiety we suffer from these types of experiences is like chronic pain. You don't appreciate not having it until you've had it. For this client, she did not carry on as if the crash hadn't happened (you can't undo an experience), but airplane-travel-related thoughts were no longer kicking off the survival system in her body. We had helped her system process the experience so that the operating instructions for her body weren't permanently stuck on disaster mode but had moved into accepting the reality that she had lived and was very much alive now. And most important to her and what she considered thriving in her life, she was able to keep her position with her company and return to air travel as a necessary component of her career.

INTIMACY STRUGGLES

My clinical work began at the DC Rape Crisis Center during the nineties, and since then, I have worked with many clients with harmful sexual experiences in their developmental history. For many of these clients, these experiences affect their ability to be intimate with their partners, and they seek out brain- or body-based therapies as a means of getting their bodies to cooperate with them.

One such client came to me because she was having trouble being vulnerable with her partner. She also had a number of triggers around physical intimacy. Much of her experience with sexual abuse was coupled with fear, violence, and a lack of control over her body. She knew intellectually that pleasurable experiences could be attached with physical intimacy, but for her, that mapping was tied up with confusing and distressing emotional experiences she'd had as a young girl.

This client had been repeatedly molested by a close family friend who would often babysit her and her sister. The perpetrator was a trusted part of the family network and used that position to convince my client and her sister that if they said anything, they'd hurt their parents and get in trouble. Out of fear, my client never told anyone about the abuse, leading to feelings of shame, insecurity, and personal disgust.

My reprocessing efforts with this client targeted her sense of safety around intimacy. Until the point where she began working with me, her logical understanding of her history of abuse hadn't been enough to override the physical sensations in her body. When she and her partner wanted to be intimate, feelings of nausea and repulsion overwhelmed her system, and she would push her partner away in a desperate attempt to create some space. She felt disgusting and twisted inside, unable to feel sensual in any way. Her partner didn't want to elicit such negative feelings in her, and all the tension was causing major problems in her relationship.

We used EMDR to target that part of her brain that wasn't logical—the part that told her she was bad and that she was hurting people she loved, like her parents. Logically, she knew this wasn't true, but the data stemming from her abuse as a young girl had encoded itself in her implicit memory network. By accessing the felt experience, we accessed the neural network.

Then, when she allowed the process to unfold with the aid of the bilateral stimulation, her system became unfrozen from the moment of her deepest distress. By including some present-day data about sexual assault, as well as facts about the dynamics of responsibility between an adult and a child, that "little girl" way of understanding her abuse was able to comingle with her adult understanding of the power dynamics and her very young, powerless position in the situation. She found compassion for herself, and her sensory reactions to her partner's sexual advances subsided. This all occurred in only a few sessions. Her life changed dramatically, and she soon found herself to be more comfortable exploring intimacy with her partner.

THE "BETTER BOSS"

I had a client who, as a manager, was deeply invested in the growth of her team. Unfortunately, she had recently received a number of complaints about her leadership. Some employees had even resigned because they felt she didn't support them. In her heart, she felt that she had been supportive, but clearly, something had been lost between her intentions and her execution.

The client's company had invested a lot in her in development as a manager, and yet, she was still struggling to understand the disconnect between her desire to grow her team and her plummeting employee retention numbers. Through that developmental training, she had come to understand that sometimes she could be overly critical in her communications with employees. She took a harsh tone, often rode people too hard, and was too quick to criticize when something failed to go according to plan.

Intellectually, my client knew all of this, and yet she couldn't stop. Her whole life, she had treated herself the same way. Her brutal, self-reflective honesty had helped her excel in life. Growing up in a relaxed family, she had always felt her parents had never reached their full potential. She wanted to avoid the same fate, and to crack the whip on herself, she had developed a highly critical inner voice so she could realize the potential her parents never had.

Her no-holds-barred approach to success had been extremely effective for her in a less intensive environment as a child, and it bred what she perceived to be a professional demeanor. She felt proud of herself and the successes she'd had, but she also recognized that her harsh, overly critical attitude did not translate into the management skills she needed. No matter how much she read, studied, or formulated, she had trouble coming across sincerely in her communication with employees. Her reputation was weakening, sabotaging her chances at another promotion and even jeopardizing her job.

Through EMDR, she was able to shift this implicit behavioral memory held in her body. In so doing, she shifted her understanding of how to treat people. Soon, she began a new approach to giving feedback in the workplace: before offering any criticism, she would first give her employees three compliments—and do so in an experienced and sincere manner. As a result, she began to engage more of her mental energy toward identifying and praising the things her employees did well. Not only was this new approach successful at work, but it also led to a series of other positive outcomes among her friends, who reported that the therapy had "softened her harder edges." She was far more approachable and easier to relate to.

THE MARATHON RUNNER

Another one of my clients had specific running-related goals. He had long worked with a running coach and had put in the work to increase his body's physical capacity. He had run several marathons and knew he had the endurance. Both his heart and legs were in excellent shape. However, he noticed that at certain times during the course of a marathon, he'd feel himself inexplicably wanting to give up, even though he felt fine physically.

In some ways, this wasn't altogether surprising. When anyone runs for such long distances, they're bound to experience a few lulls. But this client's experience was different. As he described it, in the middle of a race, he would feel a heavy cloak settle over him and be overcome with the desire to drop his pace and start walking. As a result, despite his considerable ability, he had yet to meet his target time. Recognizing that his issues were mental rather than physical, his running coach referred this exasperated marathon runner to my center.

During our sessions, we targeted his experience around failure and what he called his "low-energy pockets." He wasn't sure when it had happened, but somewhere along the line, his internal messaging around success—specifically success in areas especially important to him—had become skewed, and these skewed beliefs were getting in the way of his physical performance. He couldn't quite put his finger on the words that encapsulated the resistance he was feeling, but he described a visual of success being so very far away. As he would try to approach it, it would move even further away. So the felt quality of his experience was consistent with the way that data is typically encoded in implicit memory—nonverbally. The sensation was the language of implicit memory. And his sensation was this feeling that all of his efforts were futile and outside his reach, as well as the strong visual that accompanied that sensation.

As he described it, these low-energy pockets made him feel like he was running in quicksand. The emotional heaviness would become so great that he felt compelled to slow down, even though he had no physical reason to do so.

We processed all this emotional material about a month before his next race. During this period, he described a change in his training runs. The low-energy pockets all but vanished, and he felt invigorated in a way that he had never felt before. When the day of the big marathon came around, he cruised through the entire twenty-six-mile run and broke his previous best—by a significant margin.

Driven, goal-oriented people like this marathon runner usually only need a few sessions to have a breakthrough. Their goals and roadblocks are generally short-term and easy to pinpoint. Because of these obvious and imme-diate results, brain-based therapies have emerged as a recent resource to help professional athletes improve performance by honing their focus and perception as they compete at the highest level they can. For instance, one professional soccer team has a whole room full of Neurofeedback equipment that they use to train their brains to better perform at an elite level. Dara Torres, a huge comeback swimmer on the international stage, had used various types of therapeutic work on her mind and body to tap into the most elite part of her thinking, feeling, ability, and muscle, and return to the sport at an advanced age. The better these athletes can understand and process these moments of intense competition, the better they can perform.

YOU HAVE THE POWER

In this chapter, we've explored the implicit memory revolution and how you can tap into emerging brain- or body-based therapies to rediscover your agency and rec-ognize its power in your life. Too often, we go through life thinking we have no agency at all. We try to take control, but when everything we've tried has failed—the self-help books, the endless homework, the management/busi-ness coach—we get frustrated.

Today, there is new hope. We are now beginning to

understand the inner workings of a whole new layer of the brain most of us didn't realize was there. With this understanding comes new tools and methodologies designed to help us identify and work through our road-blocks in a wholly new way. Today's neuropsychologists are working together to understand the whole human system and how it works in an integrative way. Leaders such as Gabor Maté teach us to find compassion for the addict whose struggles are rooted in the data of trauma's implicit effects, while Bessel van der Kolk teaches us how the body holds stress in our cellular makeup. Naturally, this process is complicated. Integrative medicine must account for all the different human systems and work with them in a way that creates change more effectively.

For instance, at one point in history, doctors would use leeches to perform a variety of medical procedures. Knee replacement surgery was incredibly different thirty years ago from what it is today (and so were telephones, for that matter). We have evolved considerably since then, exploring the human system with increasing sophistication and learning how to work in a space—the human brain—that's tremendously complicated.

Our synapses encode experiences in many different ways, and this process informs what we experience in our psychology. Scientists now understand that many of these experiences create pathways in the unconscious parts of our brains with origins we may not remember and leave imprints we're often unaware of.

WHY THIS MATTERS

The implicit memories that adoptees are unaware of are becoming more of a focus of clinical attention since adoptees are overrepresented in mental health treatment, substance abuse treatment, and suicide statistics. For example:

- A national sample of those with substance use disorders showed adoptees to be two to three times more likely to struggle with substance use disorders than nonadoptees.[10]

- Studies show an average of 25 to 35 percent of young people in residential treatment centers are adoptees. This is seventeen times the norm.[11]

- Suicide rates for adoptees are four times greater than the suicide rate of nonadoptees.[12]

If more practitioners simply understood that (1) distressing experiences in early childhood are stored in implicit memory and that (2) those implicit memories *can be rewired* through nonverbal therapeutic approaches, many of the suffering and missed treatment opportunities among this population could be avoided. This is especially important for adoptees because the trauma itself has oftentimes occurred during the preverbal/preconscious years of their lives—specifically before the age of three.

In my previous role as a university professor, I was sharing some of this data regarding adoptees with my class of graduate students. One of my students took this information to heart. That week at her clinical field practicum, which was an alternative middle school for students who had been tagged as behaviorally inappropriate for traditional learning environments, she asked her clinical supervisor how many of the preteens had been adopted. The supervisor was surprised by her student's question and answered that she didn't know.

This was a therapeutic school. It had daily therapy and groups for these struggling students—students who had set fire to their schools, been violent with peers, struggled with substance abuse, or could not tolerate authority. Suspecting there was a connection to adoption, my student took it upon herself to find the answers. She looked through the student's intake notes and was shocked to discover that 100 percent of the students at that alternative educational institution had a history of adoption. Yet, *none* of the clinicians or specialists were trained to work with adoptees, knew about implicit memory, or were equipped to understand the adoptee experience. This entire program was missing an important common denominator in the population they were serving. Furthermore, they had this data but simply did not see this demographic data as relevant.

My student had not only asked an important question, but she then shared some of the adoptee-centric mental health resources that she had learned about from our class.[13] This led this program down a new path for how to deliver a quality service to this hurting population.

In the words of Reverend Keith C. Griffith, "Adoption loss is the only trauma in the world where the victims are expected by the whole of society to be grateful."[14] These students had been shuffled around from school to school and treated as delinquent, but none of the administrators had bothered to understand their lived experience.

10   G. Yoon, J. Westermeyer, M. Warwick, and M.A. Kuskowski, "Substance Use Disorders and Adoption: Findings from a National Sample," *PLoS ONE* 7, no. 11 (2012): e49655, https://doi.org/10.1371/journal.pone.0049655.

11   Betty Jean Lifton, *Lost and Found: The Adoption Experience*, 2nd ed. (New York: Harper & Row, 1988).

12   M.A. Keyes, S.M. Malore, A. Sharma, W. Iacono, and M. McGue, "Risk of Suicide Attempt in Adopted and Non-Adopted Offspring," *Pediatrics* 132, no. 4 (2013): 639-46.

13   Nancy Verrier, *The Primal Wound: Understanding the Adopted Child* (California: Verrier Publishing, 1993); Nancy Verrier, *Coming Home to Self: The Adopted Child Grows Up* (California: Verrier Publishing, 2004).

14   Mirah Riben, "Living with Adoption's Dichotomies and Myths," *Huffington Post*, March 22, 2015, https://www.huffingtonpost.com/mirah-riben/living-with-adoptions-com_b_6504642.html.

———

CHAPTER THREE

THE POWER OF ADVANCED BRAIN-BASED THERAPIES

The human brain is an incredible pattern-matching machine.

—JEFF BEZOS

Brain-based therapies access specific areas of the brain in different ways, from bilateral stimulation to eye musculature and brain mapping to electrode-based conditioning. Through these processes, practitioners work to change brain function, as well as access specific pathways along our neural networks, target those pathways, and then change them in a specific way based on a client's specifications.

So what are neural pathways? On a basic level, neural pathways describe the ways in which our neurons are wired together to create a pathway or sequence that informs an action. We have a neural pathway that says, "This is the way to snap your fingers," and another that says, "This is the way your heart beats." These are not consciously created. Neural pathways just happen. The groundwork for them is laid in utero, and then the natural process of life creates experiences that are constantly forming or reinforcing neural pathways operating in our system.

While so many of our life experiences are creating new pathways, the pathways themselves begin to group together to form networks of pathways, which are typically referred to as neural networks. To understand how this works, picture a dance routine. To master it, a performer must learn a series of individual moves, as well as their relationship to each other. As the performer practices, each new move becomes its own neural pathway, and as the routine comes together, these pathways then group together to form a neural network.

Similar data stores are created with every new experience, whether it's primarily emotional, sensory, or visceral data. Whatever the case, these networks group together a series of neural pathways in a way that instructs our human system on how to respond in a given situation.

You and I may not realize it, but this is happening *all the time* and without our permission. Either way, whenever these responses are first formed, our system considers them to be the most adaptive networks at the time. A point that bears repeating is that although we may outgrow these neural networks, they were adopted because, at an earlier stage of life, they had been the most effective way of coping with situations of that era. They either no longer serve us in the present day or they haven't been updated to reflect our present realities, goals, and desires.

No matter what we're doing, a variety of neural networks are involved. Scientists can measure the level of activity of these neural networks in the brain, tracking baseline levels for heart and respiration function, sleep processes, and even emotional responses. This active system can have a profound impact on how we feel as well as how we behave.

Through every daily activity and experience, millions of neural pathways in our brain are telling us how the world works and managing how we function day to day. They help us put our shoes on. They help us pirouette. If we don't know how to pirouette, our brains have to create new pathways organized into a network for that activity. Over time, we will have built a fully formed set of neural pathways and networks that tell us how to handle ourselves in various aspects of our daily lives: how to respond emotionally, what to focus on, where to look, where the body needs to go, and the sequence of movements necessary to execute. It's as if we have countless little complex maps with commands of how to manage the intricacies of every aspect of living.

To work properly, a given pathway and network, such as the one that enables a pirouette, must connect with other pathways and networks—pathways that engage the heart and lungs, networks that tell your legs how to push off from the ground (while balancing), networks that twist your body into a spin, and so on. Every time you perform that activity, you generate new sensory information, causing these pathways to shift and adjust to account for the new data. In all, these processes are as rich and complex as the brain that houses them, with each synapse firing in harmony to complete an action, thought, experience, or sensation.

Neural networks play a key role in creating and accessing our implicit memories. Remember, implicit memories lie in areas of the brain that we can't access with our conscious minds. We cannot intellectually find this data. However, we *can* access these memories through neural pathways. In fact, these pathways become the medium for changing and working with the material stored as implicit memories.

Current and emerging advances in brain-based therapies target these networks as access points and enhance the ability of the brain to perform its infinitely complex work, reprocessing the data and shifting the way those messages are stored. The most effective of these processes don't seek to guide or control the brain, but rather to comingle new, more desirable data into the preexisting neural networks being targeted. Examples of desirable data might be "I am safe," "I have power," "I am capable," and so on. Data such as these will help you to thrive in your life. These processes ultimately allow the brain to do what it does best: seek the most adaptive and efficient data to perform the task at hand. Simultaneously, these processes also tap into key brain functions to help move and shift data. This is perhaps one of the most amazing aspects of brain-based therapies: when it comes down to it, they're simply a targeted way of prompting the brain to improve—just the way it wants to anyway.

COMMON MISCONCEPTIONS ABOUT BRAIN-BASED THERAPY

There are many misconceptions about brain-based therapy. However, as is often the case, hearing about these approaches to treatment and actually experiencing them are two different things. The following are the three most common misconceptions my clients have shared.

MISCONCEPTION #1: YOU HAVE TO BE ABLE TO PINPOINT AND RECALL DISTRESSING EVENTS TO REPROGRAM NEURAL NETWORKS

In the past, people have felt like they have to know the story of their distress in order to get over it. They may have thought that without intellectually knowing the data, they could never heal from it. Today, we know that is not the case based on the work of Sandra Paulsen and her extensive studies of implicit memory.[1]

You don't have to know the facts of your story to be able to reprogram the symptoms or the outcomes.[2] You don't have to know the facts of your symptoms' origins, and you don't have to do the analysis. The code in your implicit memory system can be changed without the need to understand it or analyze it.

This reality is a golden ticket for those without access to their history. It also saves countless hours and dollars in treatment understanding this truth. Although an intellectual understanding can be very grounding, it is not required to heal or make changes in daily performance or well-being.

1   S. Paulsen and K. O'Shea, *When There Are No Words: Repairing Early Trauma and Neglect from the Attachment Period with EMDR Therapy* (Bainbridge Island, WA: Bainbridge Institute for Integrative Psychology, 2017).

2   Peter Levine, Somatic Experiencing, April 2010, https://somaticperspectives.com/zug/transcripts/Levine-2010-04.pdf.

MISCONCEPTION #2: IN ORDER FOR TRAUMA TO BE HEALED, IT MUST BE RETOLD AND RELIVED

Countless clients have said they were initially reluctant to work on traumatic experiences of any kind because they didn't want to relive the disappointments, heartaches, or terrors of their lives, especially considering how hard they had worked day in and day out to forget about those unfortunate circumstances. Most clients had consciously or unconsciously made pacts with themselves not to dwell on what couldn't be changed.

With brain- or body-based therapeutic approaches, it is not necessary to relive overwhelming experiences in order to heal from them. Although there may be parts of experiences that are recalled in the process, it is not necessary for reprogramming.

Brain- and body-based therapies do not operate on linear recounting or recall. During a session, you may experience a flash of memory from time to time, but that's temporary. The work takes place primarily within your neural networks.[3] The experience is different for everyone, but any memories tend to go by in a fast, nonsensical way—a far cry from having to relive a painful experience.

---

3   Elissa Melargano, "Trauma in the Body: Interview with Bessel van der Kolk," *Still Harbor*, November 18, 2015, http://stillharbor.org/anchormagazine/2015/11/18/trauma-in-the-body.

MISCONCEPTION #3: EVERYONE'S EXPERIENCE IS THE SAME

Our neural networks are fascinatingly complex systems, each as unique to the individual as their fingerprints. Because of the complex processes in which these networks are laid, the experience and delivery of brain-based therapy is different from person to person and leads to different outcomes.

Practitioners can see the difference in these client experiences with brain- or body-based therapeutic work firsthand. Some clients exhibit some form of outward sign of processing: changes in breathing, physical tics, or uncontrollable laughing, shaking, or rocking. Sometimes, the experience doesn't bring about a physical response at all. Clients sometimes report more visual processing or a series of sounds or feelings. Whatever the case for the client, the general protocols of how the treatments are administered by the practitioner remain the same and ultimately bring about desired outcomes.

HOW BRAIN-BASED THERAPY WORKS

Brain-based therapy is a rich and growing field. As one might expect when working with neural networks, each methodology is a nuanced, complicated process. However, it's also client-directed. Regardless of methodology, practitioners at my center use the following high-level framework to guide their process.

STEP #1: DEVELOP RAPPORT AND TRUST FOR THE PROCESS

The cornerstone for effective therapeutic work is in developing both connection and safety within the relationship. I don't mean general trust, but rather that type of feeling that comes from deeply understanding on every level (especially subconsciously) that you are in good hands. This is a foundation for doing this direct work with implicit memory, and the time it takes to establish it can vary from person to person. For example, if a client has had negative experiences with trust in general, the process can be longer than for a person who has had close, consistent, and dependable people in their lives.

STEP #2: UNDERSTAND THE LAY OF THE LAND

Understanding a person's general history and life experiences is very important in this type of delicate work—both for the client and for the practitioner. Ideally, when working nonverbally, a client has internal resources that can be called upon should unknown pockets of experience come up. Remember that this is not a linear process. It is also not verbal. The clinician needs to be aware of a client's abilities and limitations when it comes to tolerating distress and negotiating overwhelming terrain.

Sometimes in this part of the process, the clinician will decide that it is in the best service of the work to take time to build internal and external resources for the client.

Internal resources are things like health practices—exercise, meditation, nutrition, and sleep routines—as well as simple at-home therapeutic techniques to teach the client how to help their system grow in its ability to regulate. External resources are supports like online support forums, books, people, groups, and community to build a client's options for help and well-being outside of themselves.

STEP #3: IDENTIFY THE PROBLEM

When people want to change something, they often speak in terms of their lives and what they want to accomplish. "Instead of missing that promotion because I'm not getting high ratings from the people I manage, I want to be rated better and do things that will make me a better manager." Or "I am really trying to take my company to a new level, and I need to improve my discipline and ability to focus." Or "I would be happier if, instead of waking up five times a night, I could sleep through the night." Or "Instead of pushing my partner away, I would like to be intimate with them."

We look at the situation that the client wants to manifest or change and work together to discover how any core messaging or functioning in their implicit memory could be sabotaging whatever it is they're trying to accomplish. These core beliefs are the entry points to get into the implicit memory networks—the encoded experiences and fears that send messages such as "I'm going to die," "I'm not safe," "I'm disgusting," or "I'm a failure."

Please note that oftentimes when the targeted networks were formed from preconscious, preverbal material, we may be using body sensations as the entry vehicle.[4] For example, one client of mine presented with OCD symptoms around clothing order in her closet. She'd had some experiences before she was two years old that ended up being responsible for her extreme distress when things were out of order (in her idea of things). She did not remember those early years of her life as an infant/ toddler when her parents took her out of their war-torn country. She didn't recall even her first years in relative safety as a refugee. But the precipitant to the hours she would spend aligning her hangers in her closet and making sure each clothing item was properly oriented and in order of color, style, and season, her body had very stark sensations. Her stomach would be in knots. Sometimes, she would develop a specific type of piercing headache. These bodily experiences became our entry point into the implicit memory network associated with her extreme need for order.

Usually, these encoded messages don't manifest consciously. For instance, a woman may shower every day,

---

4   Pat Ogden, *Trauma and the Body: A Sensorimotor Approach to Psychotherapy* (London and New York: W.W. Norton & Company, 2006).

contribute to the well-being of the planet, and engage in healthy relationships with friends and partners. However, encoded deep in her neural pathways is the idea that she is disgusting and worthless—an idea that has plagued her unconscious since a difficult experience she had as a young girl. For the most part, she can get by just fine even with this encoded message, but one day, it might sabotage an important goal or relationship. For instance, she might hold herself back from submitting a large, high-dollar proposal, or she might think twice about applying to speak on a big stage. To her, the foot dragging seems illogical. She *wants* to do these things, but the encoded messages in her neural networks are driving the show without her conscious consent or intellectual understanding.

STEP #4: ACCESS THE HIDDEN CONTROL PANEL

Once a client has shared as much information as they can, we can then be better equipped to find the more sensory data that is likely an indicator of what codes may be in the hidden panel related to the therapeutic goal. This hidden panel rarely operates in the conscious mind, but because it's always running in the background, it can dramatically impact a person's mood, physical well-being, and ability to perform in their life.

The specifics of the entry point don't matter as much as

the fact that there *is* an entry point. That said, certain entry points for different therapeutic approaches are contraindicated. If someone says they have a history of migraines, for instance, a practitioner will want more information before proceeding. What is their medical history? Is the client on any medications, and do they have any allergies? Do they have a history of anything more serious, such as seizures? Depending on the answers, a practitioner may choose not to use EMDR, instead electing to use a method of bilateral stimulation that will be tactile rather than visual or choosing Brainspotting or Neurofeedback.

STEP #5: REPROGRAM THE NETWORK

Once we have tapped into a client's hidden control panel, we can make profound changes in the ways they experience their daily lives. Often, the strongest core beliefs result from early childhood experiences, a fact that was reinforced for me time and again during my work at the rape crisis center. Although each client's story was unique, involving different people, scenarios, and disappointments, the more stories I heard, the more apparent it became to me that the earlier the experience, the deeper the impact.

A horrifying experience such as rape, for instance, is traumatic at any age. However, the earlier the trauma, the more far-reaching implications it can have into different areas of a person's life. Early experiences create important building blocks in our internal quest to thrive in our lives. Subsequent experiences then build on what is already known by the brain. Adding to this, the earlier the experience, the more it tends to be spread out across various neural networks—and the more complicated it can be for clients to reprocess and reprogram the experience.[5]

This step involves utilizing information already available to the client, as well as experiences that the client has had that have given contradictory data to their system, especially data in the service of their goals. During this time period, no matter the therapeutic approach, more adaptive data is discovered, installed, and reprogrammed into the implicit memory system so that a new code consistent with supporting the client's goals are the new default belief.

STEP #6: MAKE ANY FOLLOW-UP BEHAVIORAL CHANGES NEEDED

Again, no matter the brain- or body-based approach being used, once there is a new set point for functioning, any new behaviors that are necessary to accomplish that original goal must be incorporated. Different than before, now there is not data in the implicit memory serving to derail

5   Bessel van der Kolk et al., "Disorders of Extreme Stress: The Empirical Foundation of a Complex Adaptation to Trauma," *Journal of Traumatic Stress* 18, no. 5 (October 2005): 389–99.

progress. For the client who came in saying she wanted to get better performance ratings at work and thereby not be passed by for the next promotion, she would now find it much easier to implement any communications adjustments, relationship improvements, or visibility practices toward that stated goal.

Just because someone's implicit memory has been rewired, it does not mean that they suddenly have the modeling, practice, and conditioning needed to be their own best advocate. This final step is about working this behavioral aspect of any desired change.

TRADITIONAL VERSUS BRAIN-BASED THERAPY

I am often asked what the difference is between the psychological practice of traditional talk therapy and the neuropsychological practice of brain-based therapy. In the simplest terms, traditional talk therapy relies heavily on one portion of the brain—specifically, our intellect and insights that can be attained—and operates under the principle that what you think changes the way you feel because all the different areas of the brain are interconnected.

To be clear, traditional talk therapy can absolutely be effective, and I use it regularly in my own clinical practice. However, brain- and body-based therapies use a more direct strategy, bypassing the conscious mind and tapping directly into the brain's neural networks. In so doing, brain- and body-based therapies have direct access to the automatic, unconscious messaging that controls our bodily functions. Our conscious, logical intentions are important, but if the root issue lies in the unconscious, then a more direct approach can expedite pinpointed results.

SAME GOAL, DIFFERENT PROBLEM

Choosing between traditional talk therapy and brain-based therapy largely depends on a person's goals and the origins of whatever it is they want to shift or change. To illustrate how this might play out, we'll consider the example of a client looking to improve their time-management skills.

There are many reasons why a person may find time management difficult. Sometimes, the reason is relatively simple. If a person struggles to manage their time effectively simply because their own disorganization throws them off, then some of the tracking techniques, reminders, and coping tools used by cognitive behavioral therapy (CBT) could be highly effective. However, for someone whose disorganization has deeper roots, then brain- or body-based therapy is likely to be more effective. Once CBT strategies that typically work do not see the desired results, coding stored in implicit memory likely holds the answers.

A good example of this is a client who grew up in a family that moved frequently for work. His parents were in the Foreign Service, and followed a career trajectory that took them to countless cities around the world. Each time his family was uprooted, it destabilized his sense of home and security in the process.

As a result, his early social years were casualties of his parents' professional ambitions. As a child, he often felt disoriented, introverted, and unsure how to socialize. Even worse, when he would try to get to know other kids his age, he was sometimes bullied and ostracized. Because they never lived in any one place very long, he was always seen as the "new kid" and never able to integrate very well with his peers. Here, it is also interesting to note that his older brother also lived through the same upbringing, though he responded to the same circumstances very differently. His gregarious nature served him well, and he learned to revel in the newness of each new post.

This client had found comfort in the containment that clutter all around him had physically provided. It made him feel like he had protection from the outside world with a layer between himself and the bullies and strangers. He did not think about this consciously. It was only after his nonverbal therapeutic work as an adult that he came to realize the adaptation that his system had adopted to cope with what turned into one stressful childhood environment after another. First, this coding that had both comforted him as a child and created an obstacle to conquering disorganization in adulthood was fully removed through advanced brain-based therapy. Simultaneously, his core messaging that chaos and clutter was equivalent to safety was reprogrammed. This client came to realize in retrospect that the clutter had not only soothed his distress as a child, but it had also literally helped the process of moving become slower. It was his little-boy way of resisting the constant upheaval. This was upheaval that he no longer needed protection nor comfort from.

For clients like this one, their disorganization isn't so much a skill that needs to be built or a practice that needs to be learned, but rather a coping strategy they'd used to keep them feeling safe when they felt distressed about their environment—a skill that they now need to reprogram in their implicit memory. The risk of using CBT in this case is that it may hone in on a skill or on changing something that might have been a coping mechanism without addressing the whole picture or the root messaging of safety that is driving the disorganization. Had we only addressed the intellectual aspects of the challenge, the gains we achieved would likely have been short-lived or difficult to realize, as the code in this client's implicit memory would still be tucked away in his unconscious mind, likely eventually leading to an overwrite of all of his newly learned skills.

Remember, when struggling to find success in an important endeavor, what you may have worked on as a goal and the way you went about addressing it may not have been addressing the root cause of the problem, especially if the root is housed in your implicit memory system. This is important to be curious about if you find yourself having difficulty enjoying successes in the long term.

SOUND THEORETICAL FOUNDATION

When using brain- or body-based therapies, newer clinicians often lack the confidence that a client's system will find the right way to desensitize a difficult adaptation on its own without intervention. As a result, they fail to trust the process, getting more directive in the treatment than recommended because they are anxious about their choice of therapy, any discomfort the client may experience, and whether they're offering a valuable service.

At my center, we've found that the more secure practitioners are in their theoretical orientation, the more successful their interventions are likely to be, and therefore the better they will be able to harness the full power of brain- or body-based treatments. Ongoing supervision, where the power of brain- or body-based interventions can be modeled, as well as continuous opportunities to gain experience in clinical practice, can help to alleviate much of that anxiety resulting from lack of experience. Having a solid foundation in both the traditional talk therapies and these brain- or body-based approaches allows practitioners to be better able to understand which path of change is best suited for a client and how to overcome many of their challenges.

LIMITS IN REWIRING—MARATHON VERSUS SPRINT

As an experienced clinician, I feel confident in my ability to identify entry points to coding housed in implicit memory, and to allow the client to enter and create their own experience without me driving it. However, there is an overall limit to what clients, their systems, and their bodies can handle. During years of practice, I have learned to recognize the signs of when someone is at their limit. In the desire to realize the satisfaction that comes from successful attainment of personal, professional, and relationship goals, sometimes both client and practitioner become so overfocused on reaching that exciting finish line that they fail to recognize when they have pushed a system beyond what it can tolerate.

Our human system is amazing in its abilities, but when it comes to making profound and powerful changes, easing the pace of the work is oftentimes warranted—like a marathon runner who doesn't train by just running the whole marathon but rather builds up to it in a strategic and healthy way.

NO TWO PEOPLE ARE ALIKE

There is no cookie-cutter approach to brain-based therapy that works for every client. Two people can say the same thing and have different energy, tone, and intention around the words they're saying. When a clinician opens a client's hidden control panel and begins accessing that person's neural pathways, they will discover a secret code that is a language unto itself. Just as different languages represent ideas differently, so do our neural networks.

Sometimes clients assume there is a single *right* way to proceed through brain-based therapy and fear they're doing it wrong. These clients tend to ignore resonant points because they seem unrelated or express anxiety about their being unrelated, and I will have to convince them to stay with the process and see where it leads. Generally, by the end of a session, points that seemed illogical end up coming together in a clear way.

Because many of my clients are extremely successful in

many areas of life, this nonlinear, seemingly illogical process of rewiring the brain can be difficult to understand. For someone who is used to being in control and driving change, it is hard to trust what our bodies are capable of, especially when they operate in the completely foreign language of implicit memory.

A NONLINEAR PROCESS

Not long ago, I was asked to speak at a meeting of Preemies Together, a support group for the parents of premature children located in Fairfax, Virginia. In all, about thirty people showed up to hear me speak. During my talk, I explained how distressing experiences are stored in the body, how brain-based therapies work to reprocess those experiences, and what kinds of experiences these therapies help clients reprocess.

Parents of premature children have often suffered through distressing experiences as a result of their children's complicated births. Many of these parents spent days, weeks, or months unsure whether their children would live. Knowing this, I focused much of my discussion on post-traumatic stress disorder (PTSD), how it works, the normal classifications of systems and groupings of symptoms that qualify for a PTSD diagnosis, and how we cope with distressing events, triggers, and environments. To many in the group, these were new concepts, and they had a number of questions. Although many listening might not qualify for a diagnosis of PTSD, the normal ways that the body manages distress were more relevant to them.

During our discussion, one father described a recent incident with his three-year-old son that he'd been unable to understand. After hearing my description of PTSD and related symptoms, he began to wonder if there was something more to the incident than he'd originally thought. He then proceeded to describe what had happened in order to get my opinion on the matter.

When this father brought his son, a toddler, to the maternity ward to meet his newborn cousin, the child was excited. However, as soon as the boy heard one of the machines in the hallway, he had a complete meltdown and began hitting the machine and crying.

At first, the father thought that maybe his son hadn't had enough sleep. However, now that he understood more about the signs of PTSD, he began to wonder if his son's own experiences as a premature infant played a part, as the machine and environment were incredibly similar to those in the intensive care unit in which the boy had spent the early uncertain days, weeks, and months of his brand-new life.

While I couldn't comment one way or the other on the

nature of this child's distressing episode, since he wasn't my client and I had neither met nor worked with him, I was fascinated by the father's description. If indeed PTSD had played a role in this child's behavior that day, it made for a fascinating example of the unconscious triggering that distressing implicit memories can foster. Because of the boy's age—both when he experienced the trauma of being born premature and living in the NICU and when it was triggered at age three—he didn't have the intellectual tools or even the conscious memory to look at his environment, connect it with his own experience, and tell his parents what was bothering him.

I imagined this child growing into an adult who never liked hospitals and didn't know why. If, for instance, he were to have a child of his own, this problematic response could leave him with a bad feeling—or worse—when his wife went into labor. Given his background and symptoms, even short-term work with brain-based therapy could be invaluable in helping him support his future wife.

If someone like this is interested in processing this road-block, the most important thing I could do as a clinician for the brain- or body-based portion of the work would be to (1) set up the framework, starting with the symptoms he wants to remove to find the entry point to the messaging in their implicit memory, and (2) as the brain-based treatment starts up, periodically check in to keep him moving in the direction he wants to go, particularly if his system starts looping in the process.

Looping is common when we face something upsetting. Whatever the event, we will work and rework it with no end in sight. Our bodies are always seeking expression and resolution to any experience. But for many different reasons, they can get stuck on a repetitive playback loop. We see this with brain- or body-based treatment too. Sometimes, we're already stuck in this loop before seeking therapy. At other times, incomplete processing can lead us to a point that's difficult to escape. The clinician's job is to nudge the client's system in order to get out of the never-ending loops in our system.

Usually, the strongest indicator that a client is looping is that the material being reported just does not change. For instance, the client might continually report a feeling or visual of distress in the hospital, tightness in his chest, and an overall sensation of dread. Despite continued processing, the physical pain does not subside, and the feelings of distress don't either.

While I am careful not to interrupt during brain-based processing, I also actively look for cues in the body that might indicate a client is stuck. For instance, if I were to check in with an adult who had been born premature, he might describe an intergalactic battle in his mind and be confused as to its connection to his experience at the hospital. As long as the battle plays out and finds resolution or an outcome that is adaptive for the client, I won't intervene. But if the battle seems to be playing on repeat with no resolution, I will get involved to help the client's system remove whatever is keeping it stuck, bring in one of their own adaptive memory networks currently shut out, or give them new information to intersperse into these looping neural networks.

Clients find themselves making strange connections like this all the time. Usually, it won't make any sense to me, especially if I don't have the data that they were born six weeks premature and began their lives with their systems overwhelmed. Even a skilled clinician may not uncover such data during the intake process. In such circumstances, the important thing is not to force the process but rather to allow it to proceed unimpeded and keep it moving toward resolution.

ENJOY THE JOURNEY

When it comes to brain- or body-based therapy, clients often feel like they have to work hard at getting the process right. They actively try to engage their conscious mind to control the journey. It's easy to understand why a person might feel like they need to be in control while they're processing, but I encourage them instead to be an engaged observer—a witness to what's unfolding in their unconscious.

To explain what I mean, I was taught to use the metaphor of a train. On trains, we're not in control. We're merely passengers watching the scenery go by. As my clients embark on this journey, my job is to make note of how they respond, keep them from looping, and let their system act as the conductor. I just help them get back on track to their goals through challenging moments.

BRAIN- AND BODY-BASED THERAPIES ARE STILL EVOLVING

No matter the area of practice, approaches to identifying and accessing these entry points continue to evolve. Any brain- or body-based therapy that gets the client to an access point and allows them to reprocess is worth pursuing. As the discipline evolves, so too will the approaches to treatment. Pioneers in this effort include Francine Shapiro (EMDR), David Grand (Brainspotting), Peter Levine (Somatic Experiencing), and Pat Ogden (Sensorimotor Psychotherapy).

On the client end, this is nothing but good news, as greater diversification means more options for effective treatment. For instance, some people aren't especially verbal. Though brain- and body-based therapies do require some verbal *reporting*, they don't often require verbal *processing*. No storytelling has to be involved. These primarily nonverbal therapies are able to bypass stories entirely, target the beliefs and behaviors that don't serve these clients anymore, and help them reprocess them neurologically, psychologically, and biologically into something more valuable.

COMMON BARRIERS

Many of the challenging moments clients encounter come and go quickly and don't require intervention. Sometimes, clients will fall asleep, an indication that some element of their processing has overwhelmed them and they're unable to stay present and engaged. At other times, that sleepiness is an indicator of sublimated rage the client has bottled up. So when sleepiness occurs, deciphering where it comes from is a part of the work.

The most common challenge is clients talking themselves out of a path that their system is drawn to process. They mistake the illogical thoughts and images flashing in their minds as unrelated to their roadblock and try to consciously get themselves back on track. In reality, they never got off track in the first place. Their minds are simply working something out that's not in their conscious minds.

RECOGNIZING OUTWARD SIGNS OF PROCESSING

Once we've found an entry point into the desired neural pathways, the processing can begin in earnest. Typically, these processing moments last about thirty seconds, but sometimes they go on for several minutes. It depends on the material the client is going through.

Often, this processing is accompanied by a physical component. Some clients could become tense or restless. If they're especially drawn to process experiences in their physical body, they may begin to fidget or clutch their neck. I've even seen clients begin laughing for no apparent reason. I've had clients report physical symptoms that come and go in less than sixty seconds, including headaches, stomach pain, and even temporary rashes.

Usually, these outward signs come and go quickly. As long as the path we're on feels productive and forward-moving—even when it isn't straight—I have complete confidence in the process.

BREAKING THE LOOP

Sometimes, a client might get stuck in some thought or idea. They'll keep coming back to it over and over, but no matter how many times they revisit it, nothing ever changes. When this happens, I'll use what is called an "interweave" as a way of tapping them back to the path they were making movement on.

For instance, one of my clients had been sexually abused by her uncle when she was young. Whenever he approached my client as a young girl, she would work to protect her sister and make sure she was out of harm's way. As an adult, this urge to protect manifested in both her work and her relationships. My client would run herself into the ground trying to manage and control things that weren't hers to manage. Even worse, these long hours were not even resulting in any tangible gains for her company, which she owned, because she was often overcompensating for the underperformers on her staff. She could not understand why her life felt so out of control. Her body was simply trying to work out some deep-seated messages stored in her implicit memory, but it was taking a toll on her life. She consciously wanted the exhaustion to stop.

During processing, she got stuck on a key element of her story. She had become convinced that she had made the abuse happen or that she had wanted it to happen. Naturally, she hadn't wanted the abuse to happen, but because she had wanted so badly to protect her sister and make sure she wasn't hurt, she couldn't let this damaging idea go. It was stuck in her mind as a way to protect her sister.

It wasn't hard to understand why this client was stuck. If she admitted that, as an eight-year-old, she had no control of the situation, that also meant she had to let go of the fantasy that she could protect her sister from an adult predator. Such a reality had been intolerable for her when she was a little girl, and since that time, she'd held on to this idea of protection as a way of coping with her feelings of stress and powerlessness.

When my client came up against this idea of protecting her sister during one of our sessions, it was so deeply embedded in her system that I had to talk her through it using a practice called a cognitive interweave. When I checked in with her, all she could see was images of her protecting her sister and all the things she was doing to make everything okay. It was hard to get through these images, but worth it in the end.

There is no one way to break a client out of such loops. Much of it has to do with the client you're sitting with. In this client's case, moving her forward meant getting her system comfortable with the idea of being stuck between a rock and a hard place, pointing out her choices in that situation, and starting to build her tolerance for a situation she wasn't responsible for and ultimately could not control.

For other clients, breaking them out might involve the use of statistics, psycho-education, or illuminating the conflict or normalizing something. Eventually, one of those strategies will work, and the knot will begin to loosen. From there, it's a matter of getting them back in the train, getting the train back on the tracks, and starting to move forward again.

TAP IN, REPROCESS, AND LIVE EMPOWERED

In this chapter, we've explored the core principles of brain-based therapy, how it works, and how it can be used to tap into your neural networks to help you reprocess adaptations that have outlived their usefulness. By enabling the brain to reprocess distressing experiences and adaptations, brain-based therapies help desensitize troublesome messaging stored in implicit memory and free the body from its negative effects. In short, they help you live a happier, more empowered life.

As we'll discuss in the following chapters, those considering brain- or body-based therapy can choose from a variety of different modalities (see Appendix A). Chapters 4 and 5 will discuss EMDR, Brainspotting, and Neurofeedback specifically (1) to provide context for the client stories in Chapter 7 and (2) because these are the three therapeutic approaches that I practice. Ultimately, in the quest to live empowered, the decision of which therapeutic path to take is yours alone. As we explore these three modalities, consider which approach might make the best fit for you. After all, the more comfortable you are with a practice going into it, the more likely you are to get something out of it.

WHY THIS MATTERS

Brain-based therapies have significantly improved my own life as a client. In fact, the more I have sought out therapists to apply brain-based therapies to my own life, the further I have traveled back into my own past—all the way back to my own adoption when I was only two months old.

My birth mother was one of many young women sent away to homes for unwed mothers in the late 1960s, when teen pregnancy carried a heavy social stigma. At the time, these homes were society's way of keeping such pregnancies a secret. Only my mother's parents knew she was pregnant, and they didn't tell anyone. Her own brother thought she had gone to California to study with some extended family. After my birth and adoption in early 1970, she returned home to Northern Virginia to finish high school, and no one was the wiser.

I didn't consciously know any of this growing up.

Years later, I started experiencing strange bouts of vertigo. The episodes came from nowhere. One moment I would be on an escalator, and the next moment I could barely stand. Suspicious that these attacks stemmed from my early childhood, I shared my concerns with my therapist, and together we agreed to address my growing vertigo problem through EMDR, access whatever implicit memory might be manifesting itself, and reprogram my own hidden control panel.

It worked. As soon as we began our session, a series of seemingly unrelated images and sensations came to me, each depicting experiences I could neither remember nor put into words. A student of infant psychology and development, I was able to draw a theoretical connection between these images and what I likely experienced as an infant. In many ways, the episodes of vertigo echoed the disorientation I likely felt after being left in an orphanage by one family and joining another a few months later.

Whether my interpretation was correct or not, the explanation and experience of the therapy felt meaningful. More importantly, one EMDR session had resolved my vertigo, a notoriously difficult ailment to treat. Regardless of my interpretation, the treatment had worked.

CHAPTER FOUR

CHANGE YOUR BRAIN

Neuroplasticity research showed that the brain changes its very structure with each different activity it performs, perfecting its circuits so it is better suited to the task at hand.

—NAVEEN JAIN

There are many brain- and body-based therapies, and many more are emerging in this rapidly growing field. Of those, the ones discussed in this book—Eye Movement Desensitization and Reprocessing (EMDR), Brainspotting (BSP), and Neurofeedback (NFB)—are extremely effective. Each offers an opportunity to change the brain in a fundamental way, though the specific type of change is dependent on the technique.

Of these three brain-based therapies, I have practiced EMDR the longest, having first been trained in this therapeutic approach in the nineties. In recent years, research has validated EMDR as an effective form of therapy, and it is acknowledged by numerous healthcare organizations, including insurance companies and veterans' hospitals, for its efficacy in treating issues such as PTSD. As a matter of fact, EMDR therapy is recommended as an effective treatment for post-traumatic stress disorder in the practice guidelines of a wide range of organizations, like the American Psychiatric Association (in 2004), the Department of Veterans Affairs and Department of Defense (in 2010), the International Society of Traumatic Stress Studies (in 2009), and other organizations worldwide.[1]

While research has found that EMDR is effective in reducing symptoms and changing clients' level of functioning, much debate still exists as to how it is able to accomplish this. Many theories point to the restorative properties of bilateral stimulation, the effects of which are similar to those experienced during REM sleep. Bilateral stimulation allows the conscious mind to take itself offline, bring the unconscious mind forward, and begin cleaning house. In so doing, clients are able to tap into neural pathways that often lead to a larger network and, if there's nothing in the way, allow the brain to move naturally toward

1   Francine Shapiro, "The Evidence on EMDR," *The New York Times*, February 27, 2012, https://consults.blogs.nytimes.com/2012/03/02/the-evidence-on-e-m-d-r/.

a more optimal and desirable space. Other theories speculate that the limited exposure and warm empathic relationship can contribute to EMDR's effectiveness.

During EMDR, a client can choose between a classic eye-movement, auditory, or tactile bilateral stimulation. They might look at a light bar and move their eyes back and forth with the moving light, they might listen to sounds that repeatedly shift from the left to the right headset speaker, or they might place vibrating sensors in their hands to feel the bilateral stimulation provided by the vibrations. The process of targeting the problematic thought or sensation and then having clarity on what was desired to be encoded instead allows the client to begin to shift from the conscious to the unconscious mind. As networks are opened, the brain and body begin to process the material.

Often in these moments, a client might realize that their conscious attention has lapsed and might try to reengage as an active participant by analyzing what they're experiencing. Unfortunately, this only pulls them off the path toward reprocessing their target material, undermining the brain's restorative efforts in the process. Again, the language of implicit memory is not verbal, analytical, or intellectual, so the target material of implicit memories is never going to present itself in that linear style that clients initially expect and crave.

HOW EMDR WORKS

From a clinical perspective, EMDR is continually evolving, and much is still unknown about exactly how and why it works. Current research shows that through its eight-phased treatment approach, including bilateral stimulation, EMDR is able to rapidly reduce a person's symptoms even in long-term randomized studies.[2]

While bilateral stimulation plays a key role in EMDR's success, dedicated practitioners stress that its efficacy can't be attributed solely to this aspect of the practice. Equally important to EMDR's success are its overall theoretical orientation and prephase practices. Taking on the role of facilitator, practitioners work with the client's whole system to map out key entry points into the client's neural pathways and networks. EMDR, then, is best thought of as a complete therapeutic process—of which bilateral stimulation is only one component.

What makes EMDR and other brain-based therapies so unique is their ability to pinpoint the saboteurs in our lives, desensitize and reprocess our response to them, and help us bridge the gap between mind and body. These saboteurs are not vague or random, and during their prephase work, clinicians work with clients to specifically identify

---

2   Bessel van der Kolk et al., "A Randomized Clinical Trial of Eye Movement Desensitization and Reprocessing (EMDR), Fluoxetine, and Pill Placebo in the Treatment of Posttraumatic Stress Disorder: Treatment Effects and Long-Term Maintenance," *Journal of Clinical Psychiatry* 68, no. 1 (2007): doi:10.4088/JCP.v68n0105.

and name those that resonate most. Sometimes, this is easier said than done. In fact, I've found that 90 percent of clients need help learning how to listen to their body, think about the possible entry points into their neural networks, and then to describe the resistances they can identify.

The goals of EMDR mirror those of more traditional psychological approaches. But where traditional psychoanalysis might take a long time to identify the client's now less useful coping adaptations getting in the way of their goals as well as process data stored in the unconscious, EMDR can often accomplish the same thing in only a few sessions. This is because, while psychoanalysis has to go through the conscious mind to identify this relevant material housed in implicit memory, EMDR and other brain-based therapies can get to the saboteur directly by targeting the hidden panels in our minds.

Many times, these codes of implicit memory that get in the way of thriving are actually discovered in repeated patterns of behavior. Avoidance of implementing an accountability plan for your sales force, for example, could manifest in bodily symptoms. Every time you decide to speak at the directors' meetings, you notice your heart beating faster, your palms starting to sweat, and a sudden onset of moods like anxiety or depression with no seeming precipitant.

Although a traditionally trained practitioner can guide you through the process to hypothesize what might be stored in your implicit memory networks, brain-based therapies can do the same work, and often more quickly.

Practitioners of brain-based therapies also work with clients to identify where they wish they could be. This added layer makes the approach even more targeted, allowing us to not only desensitize the saboteur that's no longer doing a client's system any good, but also create a new context that makes sense with the present-day data and goals that are alive and well.

Once a saboteur is desensitized, we use bilateral stimulation to help clients reprocess a positive belief they understand intellectually in order to also internalize it at a deep unconscious level. Once we have opened the relevant neural pathway, we move to integrate it and the new belief with support from adaptive memory networks.

IMPROVING JOB PERFORMANCE

As we've discussed throughout this book, EMDR and other brain- or body-based therapies are effective not only for alleviating trauma but also for achieving personal goals and improving job performance. To set this discussion in a real-world context, we'll use the story of a female attorney on the verge of undermining her career before I took her on as a client.

EMDR ISN'T FOR EVERYONE

I've had clients who want to do EMDR, but have reservations. Some, for instance, worry that the sessions might bring out something they've never told anyone. In truth, sometimes this does happen, especially if it's intertwined with whatever material we were trying to unpack. However, whenever this occurs, it's typically a relief for the client and weaves into the work of rewiring the present-day saboteur in their brain. Rather than letting it become another distressing experience, the client ultimately appreciates it as a conduit for powerful change.

Others have the mistaken concern that, once bilateral stimulation begins, they will fully reexperience something painful or difficult. Luckily, that's not how it works. Even clients focusing on the most difficult neural networks in their system only experience flashes of memory or experience, which generally last between thirty seconds and two minutes. However, even those flashes tend not to be nearly as visceral or distressing as clients expect.

Whether their clients' concerns are valid or misplaced, an experienced EMDR practitioner will not subject someone to processing who isn't ready. Especially if they're doing work in the darkest rabbit holes of their mind, the client has to trust both in the process and in their practitioner. If that confidence isn't there, the practitioner will focus on building a trusting relationship with that client before they begin work.

Because of this, EMDR isn't for everyone. Sometimes, that trust can't be built. Sometimes, if people's desires are beyond what is physically possible, they will be unable to see the results they hope for, even if they enter the process with the best of intentions. Examples are goals that involve changing the past, growing a foot taller, or birthing children when you are sixty-five years old. In other words, you can optimize what you have, but you can't change what you are.

To use an analogy, you could have the best basketball moves ever. You could dedicate your life to building your strength, agility, and coordination. However, if you're only five foot seven, all you can do is optimize what you have. You can't change the fundamental facts about yourself. Similarly, certain parts of your own story and abilities have their limits as well. You can't undo those limitations, but you can work to optimize and sharpen what you have to help you thrive to the best of your abilities.

In other words, our systems are adaptive, but neither EMDR nor any other brain-based therapy is a magic pill. It's simply a process that facilitates change in a targeted way that helps us optimize our best traits and perform to the best of our abilities. Some client perspectives on their experiences with EMDR can be found in Chapter 7.

When this attorney came to me for a series of traditional talk-therapy sessions, she was deeply upset and said she wanted to quit her job. Working at a prestigious law firm, she was an industry leader in her practice area and was recognized for her thought leadership and advocacy across the country. Despite this, she felt underappreciated and unfairly compensated. To make matters worse, she had recently received a bad performance review from her boss and was shocked. She had always given 110 percent, and she was appalled that they hadn't noticed the many ways in which she believed she performed above and beyond the standard expected of her. She figured her bosses felt intimidated by her and were deliberately holding her back in her career.

Because of this, she felt she had only one choice: ditch the job at the prestigious law firm and look for a new opportunity elsewhere. She came to the Viva Center not so that I could talk her out of this plan, but rather so that I could reinforce her decision and begin to identify the next steps in finding a new job.

When I hear stories like this, I try to remember that I'm only hearing one person's side of it. For all I knew, her managers could have been every bit as awful as she claimed they were, or they could have been saints. Regardless, she was ready to jump out of a plane without a parachute by leaving her job, and I had an opportunity to present her with a different path.

During our first intake session, we started to pull apart what was happening at work. She was outraged and listed out her managers' many offenses and highlighted all the extra work she had done that she hadn't even been asked to do. She wasn't getting enough sleep, she was incredibly stressed, and her efforts were not being appreciated. After hearing this, I asked her why she was doing so much extra work.

"That's just what you do," she said. "That's how I got

through law school. I was always that team player, and I guess I thought that when I did that, people would be generous with me. It's certainly not working out that way."

From there, we started doing some exploratory research on her present-day life, working to identify potential saboteurs. Because she was a fairly high-level employee at her firm and hadn't been actively leveraging her networks, finding a new job wasn't going to happen overnight. As we wrapped up the session, I asked her to spend a week trying to not say yes to everyone at work—to not always be available to respond to every request.

The next week, she told me how difficult it had been to say no. In fact, she found it so hard that she couldn't even do it. She knew it wasn't in her best interest to be a yes person, but she couldn't help herself, and she didn't know why. At least, she didn't know why at first.

Eventually, I learned that her struggle had much deeper origins, stretching all the way back to her relationship with her parents. My client said they were good people, good parents, and conscientious members of their community. However, they weren't present for her or her sister. From a young age, she learned that she couldn't have problems of her own. Any distress or disappointment she expressed fell on deaf ears, and it was painful. She realized she would be better rewarded if she could gauge what her parents needed and provide that. They didn't have a lot of bandwidth for her if she wasn't following a certain script, and that script looked a lot like her tendency to overachieve and overperform in adulthood.

It took a while for her to reflect on this. It was painful for her to realize, but her body was telling the story. Even as a successful attorney, she didn't feel good setting boundaries or saying no. Beginning to do this was like moving a boulder.

Given her background, I believed this client was an ideal candidate for EMDR therapy. I gave her some information and told her how it worked. We agreed to try to reprocess the part of her that used overachievement to cope with the rough parts of her childhood. We would especially target the parts of her coding that were programmed in her unconscious. For her new goal to help her target and reprocess her implicit memory of childhood, this client said she wanted to feel valuable, which, somewhat paradoxically, meant becoming better at setting boundaries and displaying healthy behaviors so she could focus on her most pressing tasks at work. She had long known what those behaviors would look like, but implementing them had felt as difficult as flying to the moon.

For bilateral stimulation, she preferred to go with a tactile approach. She held what we call tappers, which are little plastic oval-shaped sensors that vibrate in one hand and then the other. I let clients decide which frequency and intensity is most comfortable for them, and if there's audio, what volume they prefer. Following this protocol, we found a good access point. She began experiencing a series of images and physical sensations, each representing her negative beliefs and eliciting a strong reaction in her. Using our predetermined rating system, she described how distressing each thought was as it came up. After some minutes of this, she was fully desensitized, and we began to look at her adaptive memory networks.

She had trouble setting boundaries because the path that compelled her to say yes was well worn, familiar, and easy to follow. It was a path her system felt the most comfortable with. Our desensitization helped to reduce the attraction of that path until she was motivated to carve a new one. In this part of the process, sometimes I'm required to lead the charge. But more often than not, the client's brain has already taken the first few steps and begun reinforcing new, healthier beliefs, which, in this client's case, was feeling more valuable.

Creating this new path wasn't easy. It required her to deal with her own relationship with herself. In order to start feeling more valuable, she first had to navigate her feelings of loneliness and not having people she could count on to support her.

After three sessions, she began seeing a big difference at work. Whereas saying no had previously been too difficult to bear, soon it became second nature. When someone asked her to do something she didn't have the bandwidth for, she would now kindly reply with her healthy boundary, "I'm sorry, but I'm completely swamped." As a result, her coworkers began to realize she wasn't just an expendable, always-available commodity. Instead, they began to see her for what she was: smart, connected, and a consummate professional.

As of this writing, this client is still at her job, which has transformed from a private hell to a dream job where she is appreciated, recognized for her efforts, and praised by the same managers who'd previously given her poor reviews. By setting boundaries, she was able to accomplish more and to focus on more important work.

EMDR didn't change anything that happened in her life. Her past with her parents was still the same past it always had been. However, it no longer mattered. Through EMDR, she learned to let go of all those heavy, painful feelings in her system, and she says she's never felt better.

THE MORE YOU GIVE, THE MORE YOU GAIN

In this chapter, we've taken an up-close look at EMDR, its history, and how it can optimize your brain by changing your neural networks and brain function. Brain-based therapies like EMDR can help you in many—often unexpected—ways. During an EMDR session, we often find ourselves at a loss to describe what we're experiencing or how it relates to the specific roadblock we're targeting. While it can be difficult sometimes to allow yourself to surrender control, the more you allow the therapy to run its course, the more you stand to benefit.

Ultimately, EMDR and other brain-based therapies are effective not only for relieving and reprocessing distressing events in your past, but also in improving your performance and quality of life in the present day. The greatest advantage of EMDR, however, is that it works even if you have no memory of the triggering event. By opening up the hidden control panel in your brain and targeting the proper neural networks, you can reprogram your responses to everyday encounters without ever fully understanding what caused that roadblock in the first place.

WHY THIS MATTERS

When I first began working with EMDR in my own therapy, I was thrilled to have found an approach that could more directly tackle my own therapeutic goals. Because I understood the origins of many of my current-day struggles to be tied in to some early mapping in my infant/childhood system, traditional approaches often missed the mark on the root causes of my distress.

One time it was particularly helpful was when I was a relatively new clinician. I was six years out of school and had been offered a dream job to start up a social services program for the underserved Spanish-speaking population. This position offered a perfect opportunity to tap into both my program-management experience along with my passion for this population as a Hispanic woman. I was thrilled.

It was a logical progression in my career and an unbelievable opportunity. However, my body was having very negative reactions. Usually a solid sleeper, I began having trouble both falling and staying asleep at night. Compounding this challenge were horrible nightmares that made no sense to me. Even while awake, every time I considered giving my notice at the rape crisis center where I worked at the time, my throat would tighten up, and I would have difficulty speaking. To say I was having anxiety in navigating this transition was an understatement.

I turned to EMDR for help. Because the image was causing me so much stress—none of which I understood—I pictured the moment of giving my notice to the rape crisis center. I had been a very loyal, very hardworking employee. I had put my all into that job and the mission of the center, and I knew logically that it was okay for me to move on so I could thrive in my career. Despite all this, I could not logically explain why I was having such a negative reaction.

During a particularly long, ninety-minute EMDR session, the images that flashed before me really took me on a journey through some incredibly deep feelings about loyalty and what it meant to abandon something you felt so passionately about. Some of my images were about church and the concept of sacrifice, as well as the deep pain I felt about being given away as a baby by my mother and other family members. Without EMDR, I would never have made the connection between those feelings and experiences and the prospect of quitting my job so I could take on another great opportunity. In hindsight, I can see how they would have played a part in the host of anxiety symptoms I'd been experiencing, but even then, I never would have expected them to have such an impact.

By the time I emerged from that ninety-minute session, all of my symptoms had subsided. I was able to accept that I have limits and that I don't need to sacrifice myself in the service of a cause I was loyal to. Now, these are both logical ideas I already knew, but after the EMDR, the rest of my body had caught up. No more trouble sleeping. No more body reactions. I could actually practice my resignation speech without my throat closing up on me. It was *so* freeing. In this way, EMDR opened a door in my life and gave me access to implicit memories that had previously been impossible to find and understand.

CHAPTER FIVE

CHANGE YOUR LIFE

The biggest adventure you can take is to live the life of your dreams.

—OPRAH WINFREY

As the central hub of the nervous system, the brain actively creates templates and sends out billions of signals to the rest of the body that can affect our daily experiences. Sometimes, these signals manifest in physical symptoms that, because we don't understand their root cause, can leave us feeling confused, invalidated, or uncertain about how to change these mysterious symptoms without clarity around their origins.

Brain- and body-based therapies allow us to escape this cycle and change our lives in the process. By accessing the hidden control panel in our minds, we can target the emotional maps and implicit memories that—by definition—we aren't aware of and that traditional treatments and therapy don't address as directly.

During the past few decades, brain- and body-based therapies have emerged as a powerful option that goes beyond traditional methods alone. These integrative approaches proceed under the knowledge that the mind and body are linked. By addressing them as a complete system, practitioners are able to get at the root cause of chronic issues in people's lives: anxiety, trouble concentrating, fear, pain, low energy, and more.

One of our clients, whose testimonial appears in Chapter 7, had experienced profound physical changes in her body. Years of earnest effort to find relief from her physical pain left her deeply frustrated. During this time, no doctor or therapist suggested she look into an integrative, brain-based approach that targeted her psychological mapping.

To be fair, the practitioners this client had consulted did not maliciously withhold this information. Many practitioners—even the doctors among us—don't always operate in a full-body system perspective. This is unfortunate. Repeated studies have found a positive link between integrative therapies and the health of our nervous system.[1]

1   B. Voinov et al., "Depression and Chronic Diseases: It Is Time for a Synergistic Mental Health and Primary Care Approach," *Primary Care Companion for CNS Disorders* 15, no. 2 (2013), doi: 10.4088/PCC.12r01468.

Brain-based therapies' power lies in their ability to not only target the system that created the harmful symptoms, but also pinpoint a desired outcome or recraft a message that's sabotaging the client's system. This chapter will look at two additional therapeutic approaches of brain-based therapy—Brainspotting and Neurofeedback—explore their history, and use client stories to demonstrate their effectiveness.

BRAINSPOTTING

Brainspotting was first developed by David Grand, a New York psychologist with extensive experience as an EMDR practitioner. He first began researching and developing his Brainspotting technique through his work with a sixteen-year-old figure skater. Frustrated at her inability to land a triple toe loop, this ice skater wanted to better understand what was happening in her system. She felt she had the strength, dexterity, balance, and ability, but she could never land the move properly.

In attempting to identify the saboteur in her subconscious standing in the way of her performance, Grand noticed something peculiar: when he asked her to recount the mechanics of her attempt at the triple toe loop and he had her visually follow his finger while she held the moment of failure, her eyes wobbled and froze at a certain finger position. Instinctively, he asked her to hold her gaze in that position, and as she did, she began processing new material that had not come up in previous sessions. Old material also came up as he held the spot, though this time she felt that she had processed that material much more deeply. Interestingly, the next day, she was able to land the elusive triple toe loop without difficulty.

David began to hypothesize that targeted eye positions could allow access to difficult-to-reach material. To test this hypothesis, he began to try to locate these spots with other clients and have them hold their gaze. All reported significantly felt experiences deep in their being—and real-world results to match those in-session experiences.

As a result of this experience, Grand uncovered three different methods for locating relevant spots:

1. The outside window. As with the figure skater, the spot is determined through the therapist's observation of the person's eye wobble and freeze. In other words, external to the client, the spot can be identified.
2. The inside window. The client internally identifies where they experience the most distress when recounting difficult experiences or present-day pain points in productivity or success as they are guided by a pointer to different spots on their field of vision.
3. The gaze spot. The client naturally gazes where they will in recounting a present-day saboteur, and the

therapist then holds the spot for that person to access deeper material.

To test these therapeutic approaches, Grand began to develop protocols for the brain-based therapy known as Brainspotting.[2]

THE BRAINSPOTTING PROTOCOL

The foundational premise of Brainspotting is that we all have different spots where we look that correspond with the different areas of our brains. Once we locate a brain spot tied to an implicit memory and fix our gaze in that position, we can get direct access to certain data and work to release or reprogram it.

As with any brain- or body-based therapy, Brainspotting sessions begin with building trust and understanding with the client. In doing so, practitioners create a safe, relational, and therapeutic container with which to work. This then allows access to data already in the brain, as well as the reparative and restorative attributes of the healing system. From there, they work to access the correct pockets of information by pinpointing brain spots and allowing that data to come forward. Often, practitioners will work with clients to target something more

---

2   For more on David Grand's early work with Brainspotting, see *Brainspotting: The Revolutionary New Therapy for Rapid and Effective Change* (Boulder, CO: Sounds True, 2014).

distressing, although they will also pull more adaptive elements into the mix as well to help a client move to a more resilient, flexible space as it relates to their goal. From there, the client's system handles the processing.

Targeting the brain spot requires a combination of efforts from both the practitioner and the client. As previously mentioned, the brain spot can be identified by an inside window—which the client identifies—or an outside window that the practitioner can use as the entry point. This spot can lie on the X-axis (back and forth, left and right), the Y-axis (up and down), or the Z-access (front to back).

With a red pointer, the practitioner will extend or shorten the wand while guiding the client through an experience that represents their roadblock. The client's job here is to follow the pointer and give feedback on where the wand feels most distressing when using an inside window to identify the brain spot.

Sometimes during Brainspotting, practitioners will work to enhance the processing by playing bilateral sounds or music of the client's choosing through a headset. Practitioners will then ask the client to stay attuned to their internal process just as the practitioner is staying attuned to them. The brain spot then processes any material interfering with the present-day target of distress or blockage.

At this point, the brain will often scan for new or existing adaptive information networks so practitioners may introduce new material to help incorporate more adaptive coding into the neural network being accessed.

Brainspotting requires a partnership between practitioner and client, though much of the work of Brainspotting is performed by the client's system in response to accessing the material. Our systems naturally want to release any coding that is no longer serving us. Protocols like Brainspotting allow us to do so. In a fascinating Brainspotting testimonial (see Chapter 7), a client shares his experience and perspective on the powerful and surprising transformations he experienced using this modality.

THE TRANSFORMATIVE POWER OF BRAINSPOTTING

Years ago, I worked with a woman in her late twenties. Anyone who saw her would be surprised to discover she was in therapy. She dressed in all the right ways, told funny stories, excelled at her job, worked out at the right places, and was invited to all the cool parties. Despite all these external markers of success, internally, she was always in a posture of performing for other people.

When we began working together, she confided that she felt disconnected and alone. Her attempts at traditional therapy had all ended in failure because she never felt that she was understood. Listening to her, I suggested that it wasn't that the other practitioners hadn't understood her, but rather that she had been unable to let her guard down. Her problem wasn't rational, but rather emotional. She had to learn to let other people in if she wanted to feel understood.

Soon, I was learning about her childhood, which, though stable, was full of heartbreaking moments from a child's perspective. Her parents were high up in the State Department in Washington, DC, and in many ways, they weren't available to her. All she wanted was her parents' attention, but more often than not, she was left feeling as if she was raised by a rotating cast of characters on her parents' staff.

As she told this story, one memory in particular stood out to her. The hosts of a big party, her parents had left her upstairs in the care of her nanny. Despite her repeated pleas for her mother, the nanny insisted that her mother was busy and wouldn't come upstairs. While we may be able to understand the mother's obligations as an adult, to a child, this lack of attention was devastating.

These types of experiences came up again and again as we used Brainspotting to access her implicit memory systems and target the spots where this information was housed so deeply and viscerally. However, getting underneath her well-fortified system proved challenging.

For years, she'd learned to perform outwardly, though inside, she felt heavy. She was convinced people didn't care about her and that they would abandon her without a second thought. As a result, she often wasn't motivated to be around people because it meant she had to perform.

This guardedness extended all the way into our work together. In fact, even getting to Brainspotting required a considerable amount of prework. Because showing vulnerability was anathema to her whole way of being, we had to be sure she had enough internal resources to tolerate accessing painful memories in front of me.

Eventually, she was ready for the challenge. We found an entry point that wasn't so protected and began looking for the physical symptom that felt the strongest. She soon identified it, and her system began to tap into the story beneath the story.

While it was difficult for her to begin the Brainspotting process—which meant having to use the very vehicle that hurt her (relationships) as a means of gaining insight into herself and making a change—eventually, she gave herself over fully to our therapeutic alliance. As she did, she realized what a blessing it was to work in a nonverbal mode while still maintaining control of her own process.

Brainspotting is well-designed for clients who are reluctant to give up control. Once we identified the brain spot, the red pointer stayed fixed on that point, enabling my client to focus and let the reprocessing run its course. While I was there to monitor physical cues and intervene if she began showing too much distress, I didn't want to muddy the waters. She was in the driver's seat. She was the one with the direct access to her unconscious data. My job was simply to follow her cues and then move the pointer to other areas correlated to distress and let the process continue.

Clients and, in some cases, less experienced practitioners often worry that they will touch on a pocket of data that is beyond what they can bear. As a contingency for those instances, I establish a stop signal for my clients and ask them to use it to take a break or even terminate the session if necessary. However, I've found that clients rarely have to use it. Sometimes they might try to override what their body is telling them, in which case, I will encourage them to take more time, but in the majority of cases, clients are able to work through the rough spots on their own.

In my experience, the human system won't deliver information that a client can't tolerate. Sometimes they might touch a pocket that feels overwhelming or distressing at first, but that experience is very temporary. In the case of the client we just discussed, her perfectionism and performance-based coping protected her from having to see and feel—on a deep level—the pain of her parents not choosing her. Instead, she was able to write a different narrative for herself, one where she was able to appreciate her parents for who they were: kind, loving people with demanding jobs.

Ultimately, this reprocessed story enabled her to have more compassion not only for them but also for herself. Instead of blaming herself for being, in her words, defective and shut off from the rest of society, she was able to learn new skills: vulnerability, being visible, taking risks with people, and setting boundaries. She even learned how to disappoint other people in the service of her health and well-being, something she had previously never allowed herself to experience.

NEUROFEEDBACK

The early stages of Neurofeedback were discovered by Barry Sterman, a researcher at the University of California for the NASA space program. There was growing concern about rocket fuel causing seizures in the astronauts. Through experimentation with electrical conditioning to the brain, Sterman was able to successfully reduce the harmful effects of rocket fuel on cats. From there, Neurofeedback has evolved into the sophisticated practice it is today. In fact, the concept of neuroplasticity has been strongly supported by the results that Neurofeedback can produce.

While neural pathways and neural networks carry codes and data that help inform how we navigate the world consciously and unconsciously, the frequency of our brain waves also impacts how we perform in life. New functional levels of any brain wave will impact change on many different levels. Neurofeedback can help us to feel more balanced, more or less alert, more or less focused. It can change mood and anxiety levels, as well as reduce PTSD symptoms. It can help with headaches and a sense of peace. Any type of brain state you can imagine can be conditioned into our system over time and actually teach our brain waves to operate at a new set point.[3]

Neurofeedback is a bit different than EMDR and Brainspotting. While all three are based on clients' reporting of desired symptoms they want to change, with the latter two approaches, the entry points of processing are targeted based on what the client wants to shift in the current day, as well as their body-based symptoms. With Neurofeedback, the physical sites on the brain are selected based on the specific symptoms a client reports wanting to change. Then, based on the shift in function the client needs, practitioners target the section of the brain responsible for that change. After that, through a

---

3   W. Ross, "Rewiring Your Brain: Neurofeedback Goes Mainstream," *Newsweek*, May 9, 2016.

specific sequencing with the selected sites, they help to support the specific brain conditioning needed for the client to reach their goals.

How does this work? To put it simply, the brain is driven by chemical and electrical activity.

You can change brain chemistry by taking medication: one pill will make you less anxious, another will give you more energy, another will make you less depressed, and so on. Different medications have proven quite successful at changing this chemistry, though such treatments often come with side effects ranging from mild to severe. And typically, the results cease as you stop taking the medication.

Brain activity can be altered not only on the chemical level, but on the electrical level as well. That's where Neurofeedback comes in. In this brain-based therapy, practitioners attach electrodes to specific targeted sites on the scalp. Physically, this means finding the site, cleaning off a space on the client's head, and then gluing on electrodes that are connected to the Neurofeedback system. This consists of a neuro-amp (neural amplifier), a computer system, and two different monitors—one for the practitioner and one for the client receiving the feedback to their brain. The neuro-amp serves to connect the client and the clinician's computer in order to transmit an electroencephalogram (EEG) signal that records the brain's electrical activity.

The client's brain is hooked up to this Neurofeedback system through electrodes that are pasted to certain sites on the scalp and connected to the neuro-amp. The Neurofeedback system then reads the electrical activity in the brain. All this activity is sorted by the different kinds of brain waves (delta, theta, alpha, beta, gamma). The client can select from a number of different types of feedback to display on their monitor, and these are presented like a video game, such as a dolphin swimming and jumping through hoops, or a person driving a car on a racetrack. Whatever the case, the client works to succeed on the screen, which the client's brain knows how to do by the rewards structure of the game before them. The practitioner controls the level of sensitivity on the electrodes running from the brain to the Neurofeedback system. The client is given no verbal instruction; rather, the brain intuits what is needed in terms of optimizing brain waves in order to continue to get the desired feedback—visually, through tactile stimulation, or through audio feedback.

Neurofeedback is a difficult concept to understand without actually experiencing it yourself. Even in demonstrations that I have conducted—with full equipment and a demonstration person connected to it—observers have difficulty fathoming what the experience is like. To hear more from a client's perspective, you can find a Neuro-feedback testimonial in Chapter 7.

Our brain waves correspond to all kinds of brain capacity—attention, focus, anxiety, depression, mood, and so on—because they impact every aspect of our functioning. Neurofeedback allows us to use electrical input to condition the brain over time and ultimately create a new resting place for brain functioning as a result of training. Unlike medication, Neurofeedback can create lasting changes even after the conditioning has stopped. This is true because the brain waves have a new default level of functioning based on the Neurofeedback brain conditioning.

A client's first sessions are spent building a theoretical treatment plan based on what they want to change in their life. Then the practitioner maps the brain and identifies the sites corresponding to that goal. Finally, the process of Neurofeedback begins, using electrodes to sequence and condition the brain waves by targeting specific sites. The client's needs and number of conditioning sites help determine the amount of sessions necessary to recondition the brain to a new normal.

HOW NEUROFEEDBACK CAN HELP

A young client who came to our center had experienced

a variety of symptoms from an early age. Among those symptoms were ADHD, trouble transitioning from one task to the next, difficulty processing information and instructions, an inconsistent short-term memory and sense of sequencing, and a cyclical tic that would cause him to lick his lips over and over until they would become chapped. He had also recently begun obsessively biting his nails.

First, we assessed his needs and symptoms. Of particular note were his delta brain waves, which were considerably higher than the average person's, making it difficult for him to perform certain tasks. Then, we coordinated with his parents to make sure he was supported as he went through the Neurofeedback process. This involved constant communication with his school to ensure the administrators and faculty were aware of his condition and his investment in Neurofeedback to recondition his brain. The parents' fear was that the school might miscategorize his behavior as being disrespectful or disengaged. His parents were especially transparent with his teachers about how they could best support him during his conditioning.

With the preliminary work out of the way, we proceeded to Neurofeedback. Our first sessions focused on stimulating the sites that would calm his system. Then, we moved to the sites that would help him shift toward more

STATE THE GOAL AND PLOT THE COURSE

In order to get the best results with brain- or body-based therapy and ensure you've met your goals, early in the process take as much time as necessary to become clear on your present-day therapeutic goals. This will not only help your practitioner guide you through the process, but also help you identify the hidden control panel in your brain and begin the journey of reprocessing.

Often, clearing one hurdle leads to another one. This isn't surprising. After all, once you're standing in a difference place looking at the landscape from a different vantage point, you may identify another aspect of your life you'd like to work on. If that happens, don't think of that new roadblock as a step backward but rather as an opportunity for continued growth as you learn to rewire your brain to thrive in business, love, and life.

effective behaviors. The results were excellent, visible not only through feedback from the monitoring system, but also in his behavior while he was at school. By the end of the year, he was no longer struggling with basic learning skills. Remarkably, all of this was achieved without medication, which his parents were actively trying to avoid.

Another client opted to utilize Neurofeedback to increase her ability to perform under pressure, a workplace pain point that had left her feeling stuck in her position at a prominent banking institution. Although she could perform a vast array of complex calculations and apply sophisticated algorithms, whenever the pressure was on (i.e., tight deadlines, presentations to senior management, etc.), her well-established command of the financial world would crumble around her. This lack of ability to perform under pressure was the most frequently cited barrier to her being promoted.

She came in to treatment frustrated at this professional roadblock and discouraged by her inability to perform when the pressure was on. Despite many attempts with different therapeutic approaches, she had been unable to curb her performance anxiety. I offered her an array of options for meeting her main therapeutic goal (to be able to perform under pressure), and she chose to recondition and optimize her brain waves through Neurofeedback.

In our initial session, as I worked to understand the way that she felt the pressure, it became evident that her roadblock stemmed from a deep-seated anxiety and fear that she would ultimately fail when it counted. We chose sites on her head to attach the electrodes that would (1) create more stability in her sense of herself and (2) calm and soothe her emotions, allowing for a higher tolerance of stressful situations without causing the anxiety to take over.

In order to achieve these results in a lasting way, we had thirty half-hour sessions together over the course of nine months. However, she started seeing significant results after only a few sessions, and they just kept improving.

She was thrilled! Finally, this one area that had been hold-ing her back was no longer in the way. As we wrapped up our work together, she said she felt confident that after proving she could perform when it counted, she wouldn't be passed up when the next opportunity for a raise came around.

Another nine months after our work had concluded, she wrote me an email and joyfully shared that she had finally received that long-elusive promotion.

UNLOCKING THE WORLD OF BRAIN-BASED THERAPY

In this chapter, we took a closer look at two types of advanced brain-based therapies: Brainspotting and Neu-rofeedback. Whether you feel undervalued, overworked, unloved, or disconnected, these brain-based therapies can empower you to change your brain and improve your life.

Everyone responds differently to the different modalities of brain- or body-based therapy. Those first embarking on the journey often want to tell me their situation and have me calculate the best approach to reach their goals and attain the success they desire. I firmly believe that armed with basic information about how each of these differing therapeutic approaches work, your own system will know enough information about how you work and what your preferences and style are to have a good sense of what might be most effective or most appealing to you. If I put twenty people in a room, each with a similar type of roadblock to overcome but having engaged in many different body- or brain-based approaches, each will have a different answer for what they consider the best approach.

This is the empowerment part of the book. My goal is to empower you with enough information that you can ask the right questions and move toward solutions that create the life of your dreams.

WHY THIS MATTERS

About a decade ago, I had a Neurofeedback expert come in to teach my class of graduate students about Neurofeedback and how it works. She brought all of her equipment and was going to hook me up to the system while she explained the theory of Neurofeedback and its origins, answered any questions about the training, and explained what they were seeing on the two screens of the Neurofeedback system.

Before we walked into the classroom together, she asked if there was anything she should know about me that was going on in my life at the moment. Then, she reminded me that what would be happening for me in this demonstration session would not be benign. Because of the classroom setting with my students, the normal check-in of a typical Neurofeedback session would not be happening, but she promised to check in with me later in the evening after class.

"Well, I am steaming mad at my husband right now," I told her. "Yet again he has to work late, and now the elaborate child carpool schedule for tonight is falling completely on me. Our discussion was heated, and I had to hang up before we got to any resolution."

She thanked me for sharing that with her and said it would help interpret what she saw on the monitors with me later that night.

Then into the classroom we went.

As she proceeded through the Neurofeedback session, my graduate students were fascinated. She picked two sites, T3 and T4, that, when combined, help to create deep soothing and stability in our systems. They are temporal sites on each lobe of the brain.

Afterward, as we walked out together and she checked in on how I was doing, I laughed and told her that if I hadn't checked in out loud about my anger prior to class, I would not have even recalled that I had been angry (overwhelmingly so) with my husband at all. In that moment, I couldn't even remember what exactly had gotten me so incensed in the first place. Instead, I felt more compassionate about his struggle with some of his work deadlines.

The Neurofeedback had actually taken the zing out of my feelings of rage, which themselves were likely some variation of a repeating tape in the background of my experience that said I would always be abandoned and never be able to count on anyone, especially not those with whom I was most deeply attached (all of which are classic issues that adoptees struggle with). The relief from my hurt and anger was palpable, and as my husband likes to remind me, he has been a Neurofeedback fan ever since!

CHAPTER SIX

———

FINDING YOUR UNKNOWN PACTS: A FOUR-PART METHODOLOGY

The ultimate value of life depends upon awareness and the power of contemplation rather than upon mere survival.

—ARISTOTLE

No individual, by definition, can internally "see" what's in their implicit memory. It's part of your unconscious, and therefore, you can't be internally aware of what's there. That's simply how the body works.

Unfortunately, that also means you can't access and rewire your implicit memories on your own. I know this may be frustrating to hear, especially if you're the kind of driven, goal-oriented person I often work with at my center. However, knowing this simple fact is also the key to making significant changes, unlocking and rewiring persistent frustrations, and finally moving forward and finding success in a myriad of life's important arenas.

That said, there are some things you can do to improve your day-to-day performance and gain a better understanding of yourself in the short term. In this chapter, I'm going to take you through the PACT Method, a four-step method that can help you to identify roadblocks of your own that exist in an area of your mind that you are not aware of, your own implicit memory. This PACT Method can help you approximate the data stored in your implicit memory networks so you can begin to understand what's going on in your subconscious.

I like the acronym PACT—which stands for Pain, Associations, Categorization, and Trust—because a pact is a statement of trust, love, and safety. Adaptations made by our neural networks work the same way as a pact between our unconscious and conscious minds designed to keep us safe. As we've discussed throughout this book, sometimes those pacts outlive their usefulness, but they were put in place to help us survive and manage the world both at the time of distress and beyond. For the purposes of our work, to discover what is stored in these deeper recesses of our psyches, we typically invest only in the pain points. Those codes that remain useful to our present experiences have no need to be rewired.

Think of the PACT methodology discussed here not as a substitute for advanced brain- or body-based therapy, but rather as an opportunity to peek into the hidden control panel in your mind and discover what might be there. Once you've had your peek, you may decide that you need more substantive work through brain- or body-based therapy, or you may decide that the PACT approach is enough to raise awareness and navigate today well enough to circumvent sabotaging behaviors.

THE STORY OF THE PINPRICK

To explain how the PACT Method works, let's start with the story of Swiss neurologist Édouard Claparède, whose contribution to our understanding of implicit memory cannot be overstated. In the early 1900s, Claparède was working with patients with traumatic brain injuries, one of whom had complete amnesia. Every day, he would visit her, and every day, she would greet him as if he were a complete stranger. He would then proceed to ask her the same set of questions, and she would reply in the same manner, day in and day out, having no continuous memory of him, nor the questions, from day to day.

One day, curious to see whether there was any consistency in her memory whatsoever, Claparède put a tack in his hand. When the patient rose to greet him and shake his hand, he pricked her. She recoiled in pain and refused to speak with him anymore.

The next day, he returned at his usual time and greeted her in his usual way. Again, she didn't remember who he was. This time, however, she didn't offer to shake his hand and flatly refused when he offered his.

"Do you remember me?" he asked his patient.

"No," she replied.

"Then why won't you shake my hand?"

"I have no idea," she said, but nonetheless, she refused. Somewhere, in a part of her mind that she wasn't aware of and couldn't access, a message had been encoded that said, "Don't shake his hand." With this discovery, Claparède helped give rise to the modern understanding of implicit memory.[1]

---

1   Joseph E. LeDoux. *The Emotional Brain: The Mysterious Underpinnings of Emotional Life.* (New York: Simon & Schuster, 1996)

YOU CAN'T FIX WHAT YOU CAN'T SEE

When you're a self-starter and accustomed to solving every challenge yourself, it can be frustrating to accept that we cannot move forward without some help. Those of high intelligence and ability are accustomed to overcoming their obstacles with explicit memory and intelligence. Unfortunately, many of my clients waste precious years lost to the seduction of these types of thoughts and are thrilled to experience substantive change in weeks or months. If you want to rewire your implicit memory, you have to work with another person who has a consciousness outside of your own, someone who can read your behavior, relational patterns, and body sensations to help you understand what's coded in your system.

The story of Claparède and his patient makes this dynamic abundantly clear, and it may even make you rethink some of your encounters in your own life. For instance, perhaps you know someone who frequently sabotages every relationship she finds herself in. As soon as she finds herself single again, however, she says, "I badly want to be in a relationship. That's all I want right now."

"But why aren't you going out with your last boyfriend anymore? I thought things were going well," you say.

"They *were* going well. I don't know why I stopped going out with him. It's kind of confusing."

You and your friend talk some more, and she continues to send mixed messages. On the one hand, your friend can't say enough positive things about her former romantic interest. On the other hand, you notice that after every compliment, she inserts a subtle jab at his expense. Unfortunately, when you point this out to your friend, it only leads to more confusion.

"I didn't realize I was doing that," she says. "That's certainly not how I feel."

You've had more conversations like this than you can count, and your friend shows no signs of ever breaking the cycle. She might not be able to articulate it consciously, but through your friend's behavior, she's communicating a fundamental message to each of her romantic partners: "You're going to hurt me."

This is precisely the kind of response Doctor Claparède encountered that day in the hospital.

"Do you feel in danger?"

"Not really?"

"Then why won't you shake my hand?"

"I don't know."

Responses like this aren't conscious. Because your friend can't see how she's behaving, she can't rework it. Through the PACT Method, you can gain crucial insights into implicit codes and patterns of behavior that you would otherwise be blind to. As we dive into this four-step PACT process, remember, it takes an open mind to apply this methodology. Some of the data you get back may feel odd or unrelated. Have faith in the work you're performing, and let the process take you where it takes you.

STEP #1: PAIN

During one of my PACT workshops, I worked with someone who had extensive sales experience and owned his own business. His knowledge of tracking systems, accountability tools, and the like were deep and varied. He knew exactly how to run a sales team, how to conduct productive meetings, and how to keep people motivated.

The problem was, whenever he had the opportunity to prove it, he wouldn't follow through. He would plan everything out and get ready to implement, but then he'd wilt under the responsibility he was given and abandon the effort. This happened over and over, and he was baffled as to why.

Using the first stage of the PACT Method, we worked to identify his pain point:

1. Start by thinking of experiences that constantly baffle you. ("I always find a way to sidestep the authority I have to hold my sales team accountable.")
2. Ask yourself what you could be trying to avoid that might trigger the pain point. List out whatever you can think of—the players, the circumstances, and so on.
3. Describe the conscious conclusions you've made about this pain point.

For the business owner, his answers looked something like this:

-   **The pain point:** My relationships don't work out with regard to tracking or accountability as the company owner.
-   **How that pain point makes me feel:** Frustrated, both with myself and the performance of my sales team.
-   **The conclusion:** I'm uncomfortable being the hardliner and holding my sales team's feet to the fire. I know I need to but I can tell I don't want to.

As he worked through this, a possible explanation started to form. Somewhere along the way, this business owner had learned to conflate authority with authoritarianism. Consciously, he understood that accountability could be applied in a kind, loving, and nonjudgmental way. However, his implicit memory system was clearly carrying a different message. As a result, every time he was expected to take charge, a little voice in his head said don't be that jerk, and he would self-sabotage. His body had such strong negative associations with authority that he found it repulsive to be in that position himself.

While this process may seem simple enough, identifying your pain point can feel trickier than it should. Some find the process to be tedious, while others find it uncomfortable. While it's not easy to say, "I have something to do with this pain point," doing so can also be empowering. After all, once you recognize that you *do* have something to do with it, you no longer have to play the victim. Suddenly, you have options to change the dynamics of your experiences.

When you're practicing this first step, make it count. Remember, you're attempting to identify and address something that operates on a different language (your subconscious) and is therefore difficult to rework. You'll get the most out of this exercise, then, if you focus your efforts on something that is meaningful to you.

STEP #2: ASSOCIATIONS

Once you've written out your pain points, how they make you feel, and what your possible conclusion might be, set that piece of paper aside and get another one. Here, your job is free association. Write your pain point at the top and then use the rest of the paper to record whatever that pain point makes you think of—words, stories, people who remind you of that pain point, and so on.

For the self-sabotaging business owner, at the top of the paper he wrote, "Authority Is Lame." Underneath it, he wrote: "asshole, jerk, lazy, hardcore, and unkind." After I encouraged him to include free associations about his life too, he wrote: "This time that my dad beat me just because I lost a book."

I even encouraged him to draw pictures, which he obliged with a drawing of a big dark spot. Sometimes, I have participants draw on or cut out pictures from magazines, though I can only imagine what the business owner might have selected—perhaps images of people yelling or big, angry faces. Or perhaps he would have just worked through the magazine, crossing out every picture of a person in a business suit and drawing devil horns on their heads. Whatever the case, working with images in this way often works when words fail us. Sometimes, even getting physical helps. You could crinkle your paper up and throw it against the wall. Anything that enables you to access the murkier area around your pain point and experience is useful.

From a psychological standpoint, this regressive exercise is meant to pull up some of the deeper associations related to your pain point. The more permissive an environment you can create in carrying out step #2, the better you will be able to invoke the sensory part of your associations. This is one of the powerful aspects of many of the fields of expressive therapies (as listed in the resource guide in Appendix A). Art therapy allows access to implicit memory by utilizing the senses involved with art-making to act as a portal to the material housed more deeply in our system. Step #2 capitalizes on these principles, and surprising material always emerges.

Sometimes participants get self-conscious about their creative abilities. It isn't about that at all. Rather, it is the process of the expression that can give color to the data stored in our implicit memory system as well as the quality of some of that data.

STEP #3: CATEGORIZATION

Here, you'll be working with a new piece of paper, this time with a predetermined series of columns and categories: *body/physical sensations*, *action*, *other types of sensations* (smell, sight, sound), *thought*, and *irrational*. As with the previous step, you're performing associative work again, though this time with a bit more focus as you populate each category with your answers.

For instance, in the irrational category, our business

owner wrote, "I'm going to be sick," followed by the more dramatic "I'm going to die." After he wrote out these phrases, he commented that he didn't consciously feel that way when considering positions of authority. As he explained, he didn't know why he wrote either of those things, but because he was paying attention to the whispers in his mind, he began to realize that the concept of authority was much more repulsive in his mind than he had realized. And of course, it was far more dire that he consciously held this association with his own role as the leader. In contrast, he consciously thought holding others accountable was perfectly reasonable, and rationally it should have been easy for him to carry out.

As with the previous step, categorization works best when you don't think about or question what you're writing down. Just be honest with yourself. If you're the patient with amnesia refusing to shake your doctor's hand, for instance, your job isn't to wonder why you won't shake his hand, but rather to record all the sensations of danger that even considering shaking his hand makes you feel.

When I work on this exercise with groups, I get all kinds of interesting responses. After I have the participants populate each category, I have them sit with their piece of paper and consider it. At first, they dismiss their writings as crazy, but soon, they start to realize the truth of what they have written.

After considering his paper, our business owner said, "You know what? I look at what I wrote, and it makes me feel unhappiness deep in my body. In fact, if I'm paying attention, my heart actually hurts right now to think of it. I feel like I could cry. Yet all I'm doing is looking at a bunch of words and drawings."

By writing out as many of these words and ideas as you can tolerate, you're creating a chronicle of your life, all the evidence of your pain point and how you feel about it. Often, this can take you far back into your past—all the way to your earliest experiences with that particular pain point. And, of course, if the pain point is earlier than your earliest conscious memory, it may not make sense at all, but it will illuminate what is true in your body. Remember here that the *why* does not matter in order to be able to change it. You do not have to know the story to be free from the pain points.

Moving forward from irrational and physical sensations, now consider other sensations. What smells, sounds, or visuals do you associate with your pain point? Our business owner described largely visual sensations: a dark presence hanging over him that he didn't understand, though perhaps it was connected to his other commentary about an overly punitive father.

When proceeding through this part of the exercise,

don't worry if nothing comes up for a given category. Some people are more connected to their bodies, while others are connected more to their rational and irrational thoughts.[2]

STEP #4: TRUST

As you reach the final step of the exercise, you've identified your pain point, described your associations, and elaborated on them in the categorization exercise. For this final step, you will need to partner with someone else. If you're in a PACT workshop, this will be another participant. If you're practicing independently, find a friend or family member, or even a neutral party, like a therapist.

Share what you have with them and describe the process. Be honest. Describe your pain point and the accountability measures you're hoping to implement to minimize the effects of that pain point. For instance, our business owner might say, "My pain point is that I see authority as inherently bad, and that idea resonates strongly with me. In fact, I know deeply that that feeling has been true for me my whole life. When considering this pain point, here's what I came up with in my association paper, along with a categorized table that explores those associations more. I want to get your take on it from an outside per-

---

2   For a sample table to help you complete this exercise, see Appendix B.

spective so that you can help illuminate for me what might be a blind spot."

Your partner then proceeds to do precisely that. As they look at your pain point, how it makes you feel, and what associations you have with it, they'll start to ask clarifying questions about what resonates with you. Ultimately, their job is take all this information together as a whole and describe what it reminds *them* of, specifically what sorts of concepts or imagery it elicits in them.

For instance, if I were interpreting the association and categories sheets along with the business owner's pain points, I might say, "In your system, it looks like you believe that authority is evil. People who do anything authoritative are monsters, and what they do is scary and horrible."

The business owner might not consciously feel that way, and he is free to say so. However, he also needs to be open to hearing his partner's feedback. That person and their interpretation may not be completely accurate, but along with the exercises in the other steps, their input offers legitimate data.

The business owner may not have any conscious resistance to being in authority, but *something* in his system is preventing him from embracing it as his job. From an outsider's perspective, we might see that he fears embracing authority because if he does, then he's sold his soul. He's become the very monster he despises.

The conclusions drawn by our trusted partners may not make sense to us. Some of it depends on many of our associations and categorizations we consciously remember. The patient whose hand was pricked, for instance, doesn't remember anything from her previous encounter with the doctor. However, any outsider can now clearly see that her system remembers the pain of that pinprick and has adapted to protect her.

We may not suffer from amnesia the way Doctor Claparède's patient did. Nevertheless, we all have these pinprick moments in our lives, experiences that we no longer recall but that still elicit a strong, visceral response every time we are triggered.

By ourselves, we're limited in how well we can understand that trigger. If we don't remember the root cause—our figurative pinprick moment—then the only information we have to go on is our conscious actions in the present. This often leads to considerable confusion. After all, how can the business owner know that every time he self-sabotages and fails to implement that sales tracking system, his *human* system is responding to a deeply embedded message that authority figures are evil?

Once you have received this feedback, how you choose to incorporate it into your life is up to you. For our business owner, perhaps this exercise has been illuminating enough that he feels empowered to take the next step by taking responsibility for how he is creating a company culture of low performance among his sales team. Or perhaps he realizes that his unconscious feelings toward authority are stronger than he thought and can't be addressed alone, so he decides to work with a professional to help him rewire his responses. His drive to have his company perform better compelled him to do better, and he now clearly sees that he is in his own way to achieve what he desires.

YOU DON'T HAVE TO GO IT ALONE

In this chapter, we've discussed how you can use the PACT Method to begin to address deep-seated roadblocks standing in your way. Remember, however, that the PACT Method is no substitute for the advanced brain-based therapies discussed in this book. While it's useful for understanding your roadblocks, it cannot help you access your hidden control panel and rewire your responses in the same way.

The PACT Method provides a useful blueprint for work to uncover the codes held in your own implicit memory. You can do most of this on your own or with a trusted group of people. When I lead workshops on the PACT Method, people can get stuck or overwhelmed, so I have them practice it with others. In fact, for step #4 (trust), you actually need to work with someone else in order to complete the process.

Having a sense of what might be coded in our implicit memory can be very grounding. This knowledge can also be helpful in the search for the practitioner that will be just the right fit. However, the most significant implicit memory–based shifts toward thriving in life will occur when all of the physiological responses to the targeted codes in our implicit memory system have been rewired. Implementing a sales accountability matrix can then become as simple as any other business task. Once the implicit memory data is rewired, the physical struggle and resistance will dissipate. When dealing with implicit memories and unconscious coding that, by definition, we aren't aware of, most of us do not have the resources to access or learn about that missing piece.

Take, for example, the story of rapper Darryl McDaniels, more commonly known as DMC from the influential eighties hip-hop group Run-DMC. At one point in his career, DMC fell into a deep depression. In fact, the pain and sadness became so overwhelming that he even contemplated suicide.

NOT ALL ADAPTATIONS ARE NEGATIVE

There are all kinds of data in your implicit memory—much of it good. We tend to be more curious about and invested in changing those adaptations that have outlived their purpose and become roadblocks, but many of your adaptations are probably doing a lot of good work for you and *shouldn't* be rewired. They're exactly what you need to know or do in order to be successful.

It's easy to think of our implicit memories as these dark, dangerous, and difficult obstacles standing in the way of better performance or a happy life. While some of these adaptations do eventually turn out to be harmful, remember that every single one was initially put in place to protect you. The patient with amnesia didn't refuse to shake Doctor Claparède's hand because she was being rude. She did so out of a sense of implicit self-protection. In that way, it was a healthy adaptation.

Similarly, that forty-year-old friend who keeps sabotaging healthy relationships likely does so as a result of a healthy adaptation gone awry. If we were to probe into her background, we might learn that her little brother died when she was three. As her family grieved, she felt neglected, invisible, and distressed. Her kid-self then adapted this experience into a message: *the people that you love are going to hurt you.*

When she was three, this adaptation helped regulate her emotions and helped her learn to find comfort in herself rather than in others. However, as an adult, it only gets in the way of the deeper connections she's trying to make with others. She doesn't know why, but every new relationship she finds herself in makes her anxious, and so she unconsciously begins looking for a way out.

The point is, this adaptation may be running haywire in her adult life, but it's not because she's broken or maladaptive. It's just that her unconscious mind is still programmed with a message that's no longer useful.

In therapy, he kept returning to this deep feeling of loss and terror, but the cause was a mystery to him. As far as he was concerned, he'd lived a happy, successful life. However, as this feeling persisted, he reached out to his mother and asked if something had happened early in his childhood, something that he might not remember but that had impacted him.

She hesitated but then replied that something had indeed happened: Darryl was adopted. This knowledge was a game-changer, completely recontextualizing his therapeutic work in terms of addressing his depression and moving forward. Suddenly, everything made sense. He may not have consciously remembered his distressing early life, but his implicit memory system had been carrying that feeling with him into the present day. Once he understood this, he was able to open up a part of his life and himself that had previously been invisible to him.[3]

Darryl was fortunate to have his mother fill in the missing pieces for him that enabled him to move forward with his processing. Many of us, however, never get that. While the PACT Method can help you get close, the beauty of advanced brain- and body-based therapies is that you don't have to fill in the content to rewire the coding.

Ultimately, it comes down to that old truism: we don't

3   Darryl McDaniels, *Ten Ways Not to Commit Suicide* (New York: HarperCollins, 2016).

know what we don't know. That's why, try as we might, we can't walk this path alone. We need trusted partners who can take us through this process, coach us to set aside our critical selves, and help us recode those hidden pockets of data into something useful.

WHY THIS MATTERS

When I was considering my options for my first clinical job out of graduate school, because of my Spanish-speaking ability, I had five different job offers, and I was torn over which one I should choose. Over the next three days, rather than take what some might consider a logical approach to my decision, I relied on what I thought at the time were less concrete methods. Instead of weighing out the pros and cons on a spreadsheet, I imagined myself in each role, I journaled about how the prospect of each job made me feel, and I pictured myself performing the work.

Through this approach, I ultimately chose to work at a rape crisis center. Despite the challenge of the work itself, this choice meant I was taking the lowest-paying job in the most difficult location and with the least attractive office setting out of all my available options. By any logical measure, this option should not have been my top choice, and yet, somehow I knew that work would be the most fulfilling.

When I started work, I learned something interesting: most of the employees there had either directly experienced sexual assault or had seen what such an experience had done to a loved one. Despite seemingly being the only person with no history of sexual assault, I excelled at my work—sitting with clients, connecting with them, and helping them learn to mitigate the symptoms of their experience. My time at the rape crisis center proved to be one of the most fulfilling of my life.

About fifteen years later, I was meeting with my birth mother, when suddenly I felt compelled to ask her about how I came to be in the world and her relationship to her then boyfriend, my birth father. Trying to frame the question as neutrally as possible, I asked, "Was my conception part of something you wanted to have happen?"

"Let's put it this way," she said. "I was a virgin, and I never talked to him after the night that you were conceived."

Suddenly, I realized that those five years spent at the crisis center had prepared me for this conversation. I didn't consciously know the story of my conception, but it was very much part of my life and my story, and somewhere in my implicit memory, that data had been stored.

Today, I'm fully confident that the truth of my past guided my very illogical decision to work at the crisis center and thrive. By choosing meditation and contemplation to make my decision, I allowed myself to listen to the whispers in myself that may not have made sense to my conscious mind but were big clues to what was stored in my unconscious mind. I didn't understand any of this at the time, but tapping into this data helped guide me toward a decision that was incredibly important both for my professional life and for preparing me to deal with the truth of my existence.

These approaches, while unrefined, form the core of what makes the PACT Methodology so effective. They may not help you resolve or reprogram the data stored in your unconscious, but they make the invisible visible and allow you to listen to the whispers in your head trying to guide you toward the right decision.

CHAPTER SEVEN

YOUR OWN WAY OUT: CLIENT TESTIMONIALS

No one saves us but ourselves. No one can and no one may.
We ourselves must walk the path.

—BUDDHA

Throughout this book, I've shared how understanding the functionality of implicit memory to one's overall well-being and happiness is an important component of becoming empowered in all of the most important aspects of living. By learning from the successful application of brain- and body-based therapies, we can start to see how new realities can unfold. In my work at the Viva Center,

I've seen some remarkable breakthroughs with clients. For some, those breakthroughs meant getting their lives back. For others, they meant achieving new levels of excellence they previously hadn't thought possible. In this chapter, we will hear from the clients themselves.

TESTIMONIAL #1: SHEDDING FEAR

Before I came to the Viva Center and started to see Doctor Julie, I knew about EMDR, but not many details about it. I had a friend who had done it, and she had shared that she had had a transformative therapeutic experience. She had experienced significant sexual abuse as a child, and EMDR had profoundly "changed her playbook" about how she felt in her body and also its positive impact on how she handled sex and relationships. She described it as being different from the other more traditional therapies she had invested in for years prior. I knew nothing about the technicalities of EMDR itself but I had the ringing endorsement of my friend's positive outcomes.

I researched EMDR online but couldn't find anything that helped me understand what it might actually be like. It was all too theoretical and felt abstract. Knowing what I know now, nothing I read was an accurate description of the in-session process, nor how it would feel days afterward.

Twenty years before I tried EMDR, I had already done

multiple years of talk therapy on and off. It may have even been more than that, if I include family therapy in high school. Prior to trying EMDR, I was experiencing some of the same difficulties as when I started in therapy decades prior, even though I understood very well the origins of those problems. I really felt like I needed something else that was going to dig deeper.

I was already well aware of where the problems lay—the behaviors, the unhealthy habits—and I knew I needed to make different choices. I even knew what those choices were, but I felt stuck. Taking those actions was out of reach for me. It was as if another force was at play, a resistance to what I knew with my intellect was necessary. I was looking for something that could rework that deeper part of my being.

I was already feeling in my body that something was about to unravel. I had a sense of foreboding in my system, and the idea that there was a process that could interpret and understand what was happening on that deeper level and then help to shift it or get it out of my body was very appealing. And I knew that more talk therapy wasn't going to help me make the kinds of shifts I wanted/needed to make.

The big problem that I came in to address was this ongoing life pattern of having stalkers—of becoming an obsession for creepy men or having strangers try to grope me on the sidewalk or at business functions.

I felt a sense of fear on a daily basis and a strong need to encapsulate/insulate myself in order to create a barrier between myself and unwanted male attention. This experience of fear was emanating from my body.

Because of that, I had created a life that was very solitary.

I also wanted to address struggles with relationships in my family. I had always been in a caretaker role. I knew it wasn't healthy. I was physically exhausted. I knew my needs were not being factored in to the familial relationship equations—neither by my family nor by me. My solution was to keep everyone away. I moved five thousand miles away to create a buffer between myself and my family.

If I was with family, I would just surrender to the unhealthy relationship rules that I had been taught from my childhood and again become that caretaker, whose needs were invisible. Inside my head, I knew intellectually it was unhealthy for me, but I would say to myself, "Fuck it. I'll just do this dance for one week."

Implementing the boundaries and the ability to speak up that I intellectually knew would be healthier was extremely hard, even impossible, to implement.

The closest thing to the process of brain-based sessions that I've ever had is the process I experience with meditation. You sit in a quiet, safe place and watch memories, experiences, physical sensations, etc., come into awareness. As a brain-based therapy client, I found myself in a posture of being open to experiences coming from all levels of my being.

But unlike meditation, this therapy process asks for your engagement in identifying areas that are "stuck." The process also encourages passing *through* areas rather than letting experiences pass over you. I felt like I would "feel their fire," but only for moments—ten seconds is probably accurate. My whole system had warned me not to touch those tender spots, but with EMDR, it really did move the moments along quickly, like flashes.

Also, I was already in a lot of emotional/physical pain, so I was willing to touch the parts that burn. Plus, I had faith from my practitioner that it would be momentary and well worth the process and the temporary moments that felt overwhelming/painful. Adding to all of this, sitting in one EMDR session was *nothing* compared to the pain I was already in.

When I first began EMDR sessions, it was hard to put into words what was happening in my system or in my body. Even before I began, I had to learn to understand my system and how to comfortably let Doctor Julie into my internal experiences. My vocabulary developed a lot in those early days. Also, I really had to break down some of my own inhibitions about following what my body wanted to do in the processing, such as sitting on the floor or lying down or curling up. As a professional person sitting with another professional person, I had to learn to give myself permission to follow what my human system needed. I have learned that my body expresses itself in a very physical way. And by allowing it to do that, I have felt profound physical shifts in my body.

Also, I use the headphones, so the bilateral stimulation is auditory. In a session, when I first put the headphones on with the sequential beeping in either ear, my body becomes significantly more relaxed. And now that I have had many successes with the process, it feels like a cue to my system that my body is going to get big relief. Now, it is more open to touching those areas of my system that were burning.

I feel so strongly that other people going through this process should be encouraged to take their time to find the stimulation that works for their system. I chose the auditory because of the way my body processes deep material. I like to have my eyes closed because this helps me to go deeper. If a practitioner insisted that I needed to use the lights, I now know that would have totally undermined my work, since I process things very physically. Even the tactile stimulation would have interrupted my ability to feel the subtleties of the physical shifts I needed to feel.

I was really glad that Doctor Julie explained the most important aspect of selecting the way to do the bilateral stimulation was determining what felt best for me. That I needed to lead the decision. That my body would need to be the ultimate authority on what was best for me. The only one who could decide that was me, and Doctor Julie wasn't going to take that from me. That relational process with her was huge!

The EMDR sessions allowed me to feel very differently in my body. I was able to react to my present life in a very different way than the way I had learned to react as a child. Those physical changes made it more possible to implement the changes that I really wanted to make. I could tolerate making different decisions. I could tolerate speaking up in a different way. But I still had to make decisions to do that, and I had to have templates for these new healthier ways of operating. I did the work, and EMDR made it more possible to do.

The world feels less dangerous to me now than it did before I started EMDR, and that has made negotiating some very difficult realities in my life much more doable. Are they themselves any less difficult? No. But without the overlay of fear and the energy there that had been insisting that I handle things as I had done in the past, making the changes I needed to make was something that was possible and that I have made significant strides on.

I would also want to share that it was *so* important to me that I was well prepared for the work of an EMDR session to keep processing for a few days afterward. I have always found that my system would keep processing for a few days. I know that is not the same for everyone. Having my own plans for self-care and personal space following an EMDR session was helpful.

I usually feel heightened sensitivity after a session and always feel I have a heightened sense of hearing. Also, even up to a week afterward I can feel very emotional for no apparent reason. Knowing this may happen helps me prepare to understand my experience.

After an EMDR session, it feels to me like my body is releasing and processing old experiences that had been held in my body. Once this is over, I feel my body returning to normal, and after that, I usually have a markedly different experience in my body. It is specific. Once, my right hip felt less constricted. Since I walk back and forth to work every day, I really noticed that! I had had cramping/tightness in my right hip for decades. I had done PT, yoga, workouts, resting, so many things to try to get rid of that pain. Nothing worked until I did EMDR.

Another overarching physical outcome for me is that I feel that I stand up taller and that my body is more dense in general. This feels better to me. I feel more significant and substantial. I definitely own my space and the space around me more.

Since I coped with many of my earlier childhood experiences by disconnecting from my body, the feeling of staying in my body is a newer one that goes along with better body awareness as a result of living more fully in it.

TESTIMONIAL #2: FIND THE DISCOMFORT AND FOLLOW IT

What is EMDR?

It seems a simple thing.

Follow a red flashing light with your eyes.

LEFT.   RIGHT.

LEFT.   RIGHT.

Just like watching a tennis match.

Or listen to a beeping headset. Maybe a vibration in your hand.

LEFT.   RIGHT.

LEFT.   RIGHT.

For me, it feels like meditation. Like silence within the rhythm of a metronome. A deep quiet among the left-right.

And then you wait.

Find the discomfort. A physical sensation, a pain, an ache.

And follow it. Can you describe it? Where is it located? Does it have a color? Is it sharp, dull, or numb? Does it burn? Does it have hard edges or is it soft? It is hot or cold? Is there a flash of memory attached? A story it wants to tell?

And then sometimes it starts to move.

The backache becomes a stomachache. A stomachache rises to your throat.

The discomfort gets bigger. This is sometimes the scary part. The discomfort is likely something I've lived with a long time. A lifetime of practice to ignore. And now it grows and deepens.

Will it overwhelm me? Overtake me?

Sometimes it will.

The pain tells its story. It can be a moment of struggle, a fit of crying. I've crawled on the floor, curled up in a ball, dry heaved into a trash can, fallen to my knees, choked, and bent myself backward to breathe. Like a small storm, a cloud burst, it passes.

And then, the pain is smaller. Maybe gone.

I sometimes watch this—almost like an out-of-body experience, my rational mind watching my body react. Me telling myself, "Well, this is weird" while observing me.

The moment I realize my body remembers what my mind has forgotten.

TESTIMONIAL #3: RECOVERING FROM LIFELONG WOUNDS

More than a decade ago, I had experienced a handful of EMDR sessions with a cognitive behavioral therapist. She was not a very experienced practitioner. I think because of her lack of experience, the work didn't go as deep as

I had wanted. This therapist brought up EMDR as an option to deal with childhood trauma symptoms that had been haunting me all of my life. Prior to that first introduction to brain-based therapy, I had only known of twelve-step work and traditional talk therapy.

At the time, I was open to doing EMDR because my therapist had suggested it. I had no idea why she would propose such a seemingly odd thing, but I was desperate for change. I was a rampant sex addict (twelve to fifteen hours per day), and I was actively working my twelve-step program through Sex Addicts Anonymous (SAA), but to no avail. This same talk therapist had also recommended the twelve-step program. But tragically, because my life was 100 percent out of control, I still couldn't stop.

Finally, about five years ago, I started working with a specialist in sexual addiction. She understood the connections between trauma and addiction (such as my father's violence and my painful history with the Catholic Church) and introduced me to the idea of a cellular level of trauma. Before that, I thought that post-traumatic stress disorder and trauma in general were only for soldiers. During this time, I read Peter Levine's book *Waking the Tiger: Healing Trauma*. Finally, I understood what had been happening in my body. Finally, I understood in both scientific and layperson's terms that I needed to work on a deeper level.

In the years that followed, I started participating in different workshops and programs to learn about somatics. I explored play therapy, music therapy, and expressive therapies, which all helped to reinforce my understanding that getting into deeper spaces in the body helped to heal trauma more significantly.

I was on a quest to find healing!

The Viva Center kept coming up on my Google searches as I looked for quality resources to continue on this healing path that I was on. A few months later, I had connected to embark on my therapeutic journey with Brainspotting.

When I first started with Brainspotting, I felt so much shame about my body, my sexuality, and religion in general.

Before I did the Brainspotting, I would often shut my eyes, shut my ears, and then stare blankly behind someone so that others would feel like I wasn't really there. I learned that what I was doing was called dissociation. It was so very hard to stay in-body. But now, after my Brainspotting work, I can actually look in the mirror and see myself, which I was simply unable to do before.

I had felt so much shame about sexuality, but not in my masculinity. Before Brainspotting, I was more passive than assertive. I managed life and all of my pain from my violent upbringing by keeping my focus mostly in my head. I survived by being more analytical than passionate. I also used to have a very hard time speaking up or asserting myself in most settings.

I used to hold rage and anger toward the Catholic Church, and I knew that I needed to incorporate exercise and self-care into my regular life. I felt very invested in working to reduce body shame.

These sessions of Brainspotting have been pivotal in my quest for health and happiness. I was blown away by the effectiveness of the modality. While intellectually I knew all of the realities of my current life circumstances, I had previously felt powerless to affect the changes I wanted to for my own health and happiness.

My journey has been long and varied. While I had never done Brainspotting prior, my other more body-based experiences had conditioned me to be open to this possibility, and I am so pleased I was, because my results have been profound.

Even with all of the other prework that I had done, Brainspotting has been the most powerful process I have used in the past three and a half years.

One time during a Brainspotting session, I actually got a cold. I had had a profound healing session. It turns out that my nasal area had held trauma. I had been subject to chronic sinus infections, and through the shifts in Brainspotting, it seems that my nose was discharging. I remembered having had to clench my fists as a child to try to protect myself from my father. I had experienced pain from my eye to my nose to my ears. I also had all of this fluttering below my eyebrow along with pain around my eyes. Now all of those symptoms have reduced by 90 percent.

Another amazing result from Brainspotting is that my chronic and treatment-resistant teeth grinding has abated by 90 percent. That teeth grinding problem was something my system had learned to do to protect me from my father's violence (something I no longer have to worry about). I knew this intellectually, but the symptoms just wouldn't subside. I felt so free as a person without teeth grinding dominating my life. I am happy to report that I no longer have to wear a mouth device. That had been a decade-long struggle.

During the past three years, I have made exponential emotional and spiritual growth, due in large part to Brainspotting. I could have never guessed that I would be where I am today prior to beginning this recent journey. Life is good.

TESTIMONIAL #4: SAYING "NO, THANK YOU!" TO DRUGS FOR MY YOUNG SON

We had heard that brain- and body-based therapies would be helpful for our son, who was struggling with impulsiveness. Julie had mentioned to me previously about how successful these approaches had been for her own children, and because we knew and trusted Julie, we decided to give it a try.

We had been somewhat open to pursuing brain- or body-based therapies before, but finding a practitioner whom we knew and trusted—and had personal experiences and success working with people like my son—helped us feel more comfortable pursuing this path.

Specifically, our goal in this work was to help our son better focus and manage his impulses. We found studies in Germany that found great success in Neurofeedback for ADHD treatment and decided that was the approach we would pursue.

Our son loved his sessions! He described it as playing video games with his brain and was sad when his treatments ended. The differences in his beta brain waves before and after were remarkable. He learned to train and channel his mind in ways we didn't think possible.

More important than any of that was whether the sessions

worked. After the Neurofeedback, our son was much better able to concentrate and control his impulses. His relationships to school administrators and educators dramatically improved and—most important to me—he did not have to take the ADHD medication that the school administrators had been strongly encouraging.

The fact that we could avoid the medications for our son, which we had always been opposed to, was an accomplishment that I feel very grateful for. Today, our son is doing well. We're confident his Neurofeedback sessions are the reason why, and I'm grateful to have had someone like Julie guide us through the process.

WHY THIS MATTERS

For an adoptee like me with a chasm of unknown memories from before my adoption, the data stored in implicit memory has a different meaning. It can create answers, open doors, and heal so many significant stressors that I experience. I consider myself one of the lucky ones to know and be able to take advantage of so many life-changing treatment modalities. I am fully aware of the suffering of my community.

As a university professor teaching in a master's program for clinical social work for over ten years, I would teach a year-long course that corresponded to a practicum experience for the graduate students. With teaching this course came the responsibility of performing site visits for each of my students.

One such site visit was for a student doing her practicum at St. Ann's, a maternity home for young single mothers. It had alternative housing arrangements for the women, which included the ability to continue with their high school education while receiving prenatal care and education about childbirth. At St. Ann's, these moms would stay until their babies were born and then return to their previous lives without their babies once they were discharged from the hospital.

While on the site visit, I met with my student's supervisor and talked about her progress and her learning opportunities for the remainder of her time with St. Ann's. After our meeting, my student offered to take me on a tour of the premises. I saw the medical area, the young women's sleeping quarters, and something I didn't expect to see: the area where the newborn babies returned after their hospital stay, which was composed of two large rooms with about ten cribs per room, all filled with young ones.

Since I am transparent with all of my students about my identity as an adoptee as well as my affinity for teaching adoptee-centric mental health practices, it came as no surprise to her when I told her I was having a strong reaction to seeing the babies in their cribs, lined up one by one. I knew from my birth mother and the adoption records that I had been in an orphanage for the first two months of my life before being adopted. Standing there now, however, I felt more than simple sadness for those little ones, all they had lost, and the time they were forced to spend without a family. I was getting a pounding headache, and I started to feel light-headed.

I said goodbye to my student and took a moment outside before getting back into my car. I called my birth mother and asked a question I had never thought to ask before: "Do you know the name of the orphanage in DC where I went after I was born?"

"St. Ann's," she replied without hesitation.

Once again, the sensory data had been there in my implicit memory all along. My body felt all the distress that environment had on my young little self. My system had so much to tell me about the distressing times of my early infant life. I was excited to tap into more data I could process out of my system in my own therapy. Further, I was grateful for the openness of my birth mom to share everything. Not every adoptee in reunion is so fortunate.

In this book, I have explained repeatedly that the story itself is not necessary for healing. This is absolutely true and important to remember, as we often think that, unless we know every detail of our story, our suffering will never end and we will remain beyond repair. That said, having the story of the whereabouts of my first months of life and understanding the reason behind why I likely felt so overwhelmed and tense while visiting the babies at St. Ann's certainly helped me to feel much more grounded in my own sanity, and it opened new doors for me to work on myself.

CONCLUSION

LIVING EMPOWERED (THE ONLY WAY TO LIVE)

Right now, you are holding so many possibilities to thrive in new and exciting ways in your life. By better understanding those moments when it seemed impossible to accomplish your heart's desire as moments where maybe implicit memory was the culprit, there are new opportunities in front of you. Now that you understand how your brain's implicit memory can be rewired (and what implicit memory is), why not get out there and start thriving or thrive even more in business, love, and life?

About ten years before I wrote this book, I was teaching the second-year psychotherapy track in a master's program for social work. From fall to spring, this coursework correlated with students' practicums doing clinical work at local organizations. The students would then take these real-world experiences and discuss them in my class. We would talk about certain clinical techniques when working with clients, and then they would apply all the theory they were learning in their master's program to their practicum experience.

After one classroom session, a particularly distraught-looking student approached me with a question. Her voice was trembling, and I could tell she was on the verge of crying. When I asked what was wrong, she told me about a conversation she'd had with another professor, an esteemed leader in his field. Apparently, he had discouraged her from starting a private practice after graduating, saying that she needed at least fifteen years of experience before anyone would want to come see her.

"Is that true?" she asked. "I spent all this money on this program so I could go into clinical practice on my own eventually. But this professor told me that I would have to work all these other case management jobs before I could ever hope to be successful on my own."

"Look at your source," I replied. "This person is a lifelong academic. He's very good at what he does, but his job is research-focused. He doesn't practice in a clinical setting."

I'm sure this professor didn't mean to be discouraging or

to upset the student. It was just that his perspective was limited and was based entirely off his own life trajectory. Fortunately, I assured her, what he had told her wasn't true. My own path had been much different than what he described, and so had the paths of many other fellow clinicians that I knew. This professor may have had good intentions, but when it came to this student's professional life, he had no business telling her what she could and could not do.

I think of this conversation often when I'm working with clients. When they first come to me, many of them have been dealt similar blows by friends, loved ones, or even themselves. Maybe they're told they're hopeless procrastinators who are doomed to put important things off forever. Maybe they have been told that they've tried everything they can to address their depression, and since none of it worked, they're simply out of options. Or maybe they have been told they are too old and have already reached their peak performance. They have run their best marathon, even though they feel certain they have a better run inside them.

Whatever the case, it's not true.

Whatever you've heard, whatever people tell you, or whatever you might tell yourself, before you surrender to that narrative and accept a lesser life, I encourage you to consider the source.

Your brain is the control center not only of your body but also of your whole experience. And thanks to the concept of neuroplasticity, we know that our brains can change. How we live in and experience the world is only limited by what we perceive to be true.

Just ask my social work student. Years after our conversation, I received a pleasant surprise in my inbox. As she explained, our conversation that day had been a pivotal moment in her life. Afterward, she started looking at everything differently, and that difference empowered her to stay on her clinical track and eventually go into practice on her own, and in far less than fifteen years.

That's what empowerment is all about.

Remember, our bodies are amazing. By learning about how they work and how they can be updated and modified to get us to our desires and dreams for our lives, we have the opportunity to grow into the most promising version of ourselves. As this book draws to a close and you set out on your own journey, here are a few final bits of advice to keep in mind.

YOUR BODY IS ONLY TRYING TO HELP

Even data that is stored deep in our unconscious as part of our implicit memory system is there for a reason—a reason that served an important purpose when it was first encoded. However, as we move through our lives, that very same adaptation can become a roadblock between us and our objectives. Maybe the roadblock appears in the form of nausea when you're getting ready to give a presentation. Maybe it causes you to shirk your responsibilities and sabotage yourself right when you're up for a big promotion. Whatever the case, whenever these roadblocks appear, they often leave us feeling confused, bewildered, and helpless.

Often, we don't know where these adaptations came from or why they're still persisting ten, fifteen, or even thirty years or more down the road. As someone who has worked with victims of sexual abuse and sexual assault for decades, I've seen firsthand the kinds of messaging these adaptations can produce and what that can mean for a person's day-to-day life years removed from the experience. Going to a party, starting a new relationship, even maintaining old relationships all become more difficult when a message deeply encoded within you is screaming to you that you're in danger. You may not understand why, but suddenly you find yourself blowing off social activities and sabotaging relationships even when no danger truly exists.

In these moments, many might call you dysfunctional, but in reality, it's just your body's way of keeping you from being hurt, even if you "know" that there is really no danger around. Brain- and body-based therapies teach us to dig deeper, that underneath everything, there is always an adaptive purpose for whatever roadblock we may encounter. By understanding and respecting that our bodies work this way, we can start to harness the new possibilities available through brain- or body-based therapies and newer technologies in the field of neuropsychology.

IMPLICIT MEMORY ISN'T LOGICAL—IT'S SENSORY

Understanding that the key to great success, productivity, or happiness in life can now be attained and understanding how that can be accomplished are the first steps toward more efficiently and effectively walking in the path you desire. When we keep trying to overcome what is encoded in our implicit memory with words and intellect, the resultant path is one that only leads to the frustration of repeated failure.

Remember, implicit memory is neither formed nor changed through the linear construct of academic learning and logic. In other words, it is irrational and without reason. By speaking to your implicit memory system in the right language—the language of sensory input—we can open many, many possibilities to change the trajectory of our lives for good. To accomplish this, however, we can't go it alone. We must seek the help of others if we want to move forward.

For many of you reading this book, this can be a difficult truth to accept. On the never-ending quest to be our best selves, we've become accustomed to overcoming an obstacle—whether external or internal—with logic. Sadly, with implicit memory, it doesn't work that way. For instance, say your goal is to lose fifty pounds. You've read countless books on health and weight loss, and you know exactly how to execute your plan. However, with every attempt, your efforts get derailed, and you're at a loss as to why. After all, you're smart, successful, and unstoppable in other areas of your life, so why do you keep struggling here?

Simply put, you're speaking the language of logic, not of implicit memory. The more you insist on approaching your most persistent roadblocks this way, the more you'll be met with frustration and failure.

To "talk" to implicit memory, it has to be sensory. It has to be tactile. It has to be visceral. When working directly with clients on their implicit memory systems, I've seen this manifest in a number of ways. One client would report having a headache for several minutes and then report a sensation as if it's shrinking. Another client would experience redness and swelling around her throat.

Still another would describe seeing a nonsensical field of colors and patterns that somehow felt like they all fit together. In truth, it *does* all fit together, even if it doesn't make sense to us. All those visual and physical inputs we're experiencing are our bodies recoding an old adaptation into something new and useful. When you speak to your implicit memory system in the correct language of the senses, you can begin to unlock the powerful potential lying inside you.

NOT EVERY PRACTITIONER IS THE SAME

This is an important point to keep in mind when considering a practitioner of brain- or body-based therapy. Often, I will hear clients say something like "My past therapist in Ohio was recently trained in EMDR and then wanted to practice it with me, but it didn't really work, so I don't know if I want to try it again."

These concerns are valid. Brain-based therapy is extremely complicated work. Skilled brain-based practitioners are fully licensed in their field. They have a license to practice mental health and a deep body of knowledge earned through a master's or PhD program.

Skilled practitioners are trained to help clients navigate parts of the mind that are neither logical nor linear. This is important because proficiency is essential. Administering a Brainspotting or other brain- or body-based therapeutic approach is something of an art in addition to a science. When newer practitioners attempt to interject themselves into the process too much, the good work being performed by the client can be interrupted and less impactful to their therapeutic goals. Years in practice, as well as level of certification or years working with a particular therapeutic modality, can be good indicators of a practitioner's skill level.

Hopefully you've learned a lot of interesting information about your body and implicit memory—and a world of brain- and body-based therapies that, before now, you may not have heard of. Perhaps as you read through, some of this content resonated with you. You realized, *Hey, I have experienced roadblocks that have felt elusive and confusing at times too,* and you're interested in exploring one or two of the brain- or body-based therapies described here.

If so, great! I wrote this book to empower you to explore new possibilities so that you can thrive in business, love, and life. The next step, then, is to find a practitioner who's a good fit for you and your needs.

When considering a practitioner for brain- or body-based therapy, here are some questions to ask of a potential clinician:

- **How many years have you been a practicing clinician?** Your practitioner's experience level absolutely matters in ensuring a successful outcome. What your practitioner responds to (or what they're trained to respond to) will vary based on their level of experience.
- **Are you certified?** The certification process for certain modalities takes years—two full years of training, a certain number of hours of work with patients, and countless taped sessions and supervisory hours. If, after all that, you demonstrate a high level of competency, a high-level practitioner will certify your work by testifying that you are practicing a given brain- or body-based approach properly. This rigorous certification process is in place to protect you. Avoid working with practitioners who aren't properly certified.
- **What is your area of expertise?** For instance, my area of expertise is in trauma, often with adults who were adopted as young children and with survivors of sexual violence. I apply my knowledge of brain-based therapy toward helping this particular population. Another practitioner might focus on sexual dysfunction or relationship roadblocks, while another might focus on peak performance or managerial skills. It may be important to you to find someone who can help you find your roadblock. Just ask for that skill.

EMDR, Brainspotting, Neurofeedback, and all the other

brain- or body-based therapies that tap into our bodies' wisdom discussed in Appendix A hinge on the relational aspect of the experience. In testimonial #2 in the previous chapter, a former client likened her own experience to a "burn." Others experience the process very differently. Ultimately, the unpredictable nature of the experience is why working with a skilled practitioner is so essential. Clients need to feel comfortable with who they're working with. They need to trust that the practitioner knows what they're doing and can guide the patient through sometimes confusing and conflicting experiences.

Practitioners use a variety of tools in these various therapeutic approaches. The most important tool of all, however, is the relationship. During a therapy session, the body begins to unwind, processing implicit memories and rewiring adaptations that could have been a part of a person's psyche for twenty-five years or more. It's essential, then, to build a trusting practitioner/client relationship because, ultimately, that trust forms the cornerstone of the work.

TAKE CONTROL

Finally, as we conclude, my final message is simple: don't give up.

Those saboteurs in our minds are tricky and persistent.

No matter how much you might want something for yourself, they have a way of sabotaging those efforts again and again despite your ability, knowledge, and desire for something different.

That's when it's easy to give up, to tell ourselves—or to let others tell us—that we're simply no good at management, that we'll always be depressed, or that we're never going to have another good night's sleep again.

Don't accept that.

Empowerment is about arming yourself with knowledge. It's about digging deeper when you suspect that things aren't always what they seem. It's about not accepting a roadblock as an inherent, if regrettable, part of your personality.

With this book, my hope is to present you with another path, to teach you that hope is *never* lost, and that there's always another way. Again, our bodies are amazing. Our brains, our neural networks, and our outdated adaptations can all be modified and changed.

Every day, the world of neuropsychology presents us with new possibilities, opening new frontiers into how the mind works and how it can work to our advantage. In over two and a half decades practicing brain-based therapy, I have seen thousands of people step out of their old ways of being and into a new reality, a reality they were often told their whole lives was impossible.

This is a rallying cry against the impossible—and your moment to choose to live empowered.

APPENDIX A

ADDITIONAL RESOURCES FOR ACCESSING IMPLICIT MEMORY

NONVERBAL APPROACHES TO CHANGE

Now that you've read this book, you know how your implicit memory system works and how the three approaches described in this book can help you live a more empowered life. However, those three approaches aren't the only ways to impact and change what is stored or accessed in our implicit memory networks.

In fact, as you'll see from the following chart, the possibilities for working with the data stored in implicit memory are vast and nuanced. Take a moment to look this chart over, considering which approach you might want to explore further and what local resources might be available to you.

RESOURCE	DESCRIPTION	LINKS	BENEFITS
The Resilient Brain Project	A free online mental health resource aimed at empowering users with their mental health while normalizing and destigmatizing common mental health struggles.	https://resilientbrainproject.com/	This online portal contains hundreds of free hands-on resources and tools that can support making changes to implicit memory and guide allies of a person who is struggling.
Eye Movement Desensitization and Reprocessing (EMDR)	A brain-based therapeutic system that incorporates bilateral stimulation of the right and left sides of the brain to access neural networks and create new adaptive neural pathways.	www.EMDRIA.org	Access preverbal, preconscious material housed in implicit memory. Shift the terror state. Change negative cognitions through body-based protocols.
Neurofeedback (NFB)	A sophisticated brain-conditioning therapeutic approach utilizing electrical inputs to optimize desired brain function.	www.eegspectrum.com/ intro-to-neurofeedback/	Adjust the brain's resting state. Lower frequencies correlated to stress response. Increase focus and attention.
Brainspotting	A brain-based treatment method that directly accesses pockets of experience stored in the brain (brain spots) for process and release.	https://brainspotting.com	Brainspotting can target material housed in implicit memory without words and allows the body to reprocess sources of fear, pain, or distress.

RESOURCE	DESCRIPTION	LINKS	BENEFITS
Somatic Experiencing (SE)	This is a body-oriented therapeutic treatment approach that is targeted to release emotional, psychological, and biological stress in the body.	www.traumahealing.org	SE leverages the body's ability to access and release experiences that go beyond conscious thought. By incorporating many different body-based techniques that involve movements, unresolved experience can be processed.
Sensorimotor Psychotherapy (SP)	This is a comprehensive therapeutic modality combining somatic therapies with psychotherapy with the aim of healing the disconnection between the mind and the body.	www.sensorimotorpsychotherapy.org	SP works with movement and the body to integrate and process distressing material that is stored in the body and repeating its felt experience over and over. Effective for accessing nonverbal experience.
Expressive Therapies	These include many different therapeutic forms of expression not necessarily dependent on words for therapeutic benefit: art, music, dance, drama, writing, and other creative processes.	www.ieata.org www.arttherapy.org www.musictherapy.org www.nadta.org www.poetrytherapy.org	Can directly access preverbal and preconscious experiences that are often trapped in implicit memory (stored in the unconscious).

RESOURCE	DESCRIPTION	LINKS	BENEFITS
Mindfulness-Based Therapies	Including mindfulness, meditation, and specific therapeutic approaches: mindfulness-based stress reduction, mindfulness-based cognitive therapy.	www.mbct.com www.mindfullivingprograms.com www.how-to-meditate.org www.umassmed.edu/cfm/ mindfulness-based-programs/	These approaches allow the nervous system to downregulate into the parasympathetic response state by cueing the brain into a posture of observation.
Acupuncture	Rooted in traditional Chinese Medicine stemming back over 2,500 years. Utilizes needles in specific points along the body's meridians to shift states.	www.acupuncture.com	Can use the sympathetic protocol to rebalance the nervous system and get out of a fight/flight response pattern (points on a specific neuromuscular pathway).
Integrative Manual Therapy (IMT)	This is a unique and sophisticated system of hands-on treatment that uses structural and functional approaches to treat the entire human system down to the cellular level.	www.imtassociation.org	Excellent for treating emotional distress stored in the body, particularly in identifying and releasing cellular memory. IMT has specific templates for working with the emotional body.
Therapeutic Yoga	Yoga is a spiritual, physical, and mental practice that has been traced back almost 3,000 years. There are now a variety of schools of therapeutic yoga that are specifically designed to work with trauma.	www.yogajournal.com www.pryt.com www.yoganidranetwork.org	Can help to restore balance in the whole human system and reduce symptoms of distress that can emanate from data in implicit memory. Can also incorporate restorative healing breath work.

RESOURCE	DESCRIPTION	LINKS	BENEFITS
Craniosacral Therapy	Uses light touch to release restriction in soft tissue (fascia) surrounding the central nervous system (brain/spinal cord).	www.upledger.com	Reduce the stress response held in the body. Can alleviate symptoms of chronic pain. Release deeply held emotional trauma.
Energy Therapies	These therapies work with energetic disruptions in our body and are very gentle approaches to healing.	www.emofree.com www.reiki.org	These therapies can help to reduce hypervigilance and anxiety. Also can rebalance the nervous system.

Important Note: Discovering and working with material stored in implicit memory is in a period of exciting growth. This table is not exhaustive, and there are many newer therapeutic approaches being developed and researched for their effectiveness at facilitating healing and change in our human system. This table is not an endorsement of these approaches, but rather it offers a starting point to empower you on your own research into changing data stored in your own implicit memory.

APPENDIX B

PACT METHODOLOGY—CATEGORIZATION TABLE (STEP #3)

To categorize and get the full benefit from this step, make sure to give ample time to record every whisper that comes into your consciousness in the appropriate column based on your associations from step #2.

PACT METHODOLOGY CATEGORIZATION TABLE

BODY/PHYSICAL SENSATION	ACTIONS	SMELLS	SIGHTS	SOUNDS	THOUGHTS	IRRATIONAL IDEAS

ACKNOWLEDGMENTS

This book is a product of all of the challenging life experiences that fueled my passion to understand how the human system works and the significant players that got me through.

To my parents, Jackie and Mondo, and my first mother, Sandy. The tragic beginnings of my life are things I would wish on no one. However, they have contributed so significantly to my desire to understand how to bridge the great divide of distress and joy and how to bring that knowledge to others, particularly my fellow adoptees struggling to step out of what is termed "the fog," which I have come to know through my trauma expertise as a dissociated way of living.

Also of significance are the important therapists that

brought brain-based therapies to life for me and introduced them as great resources in my own personal struggles. In this regard, a special thank you to Deany Laliotis and Tom Berg, as well as my other great teachers that have taught me so much about trauma, healing, and implicit memory: Dr. Elizabeth Smith, Dr. Cathie Gray, Dr. Joseph Shields, and Dr. Sandra Paulsen.

Then there are my generous colleagues dedicated to making this world a more empowered place. Especially those who put their talents, insights, or connections into making this book what it is—namely Lilly McGee, Georgiana Mora, Alina McClerklin, Susan Fago, Sara Mindel, Nicole Burton, Atieno Williams, Lisa Klein, Steve Sawyer, Monica Freedman, Melanie Spring, Nancy Verrier, Regina Tosca, Chas Hoppe, and so many others.

And of course, thank you to those who support and sacrifice regularly for my passions and my desire to bring what I know to the public—my wonderful, supportive husband, Grover; our four children, Landon, Maya, Wes, and Lucas; and our two divine canines, Santa and Bailey, who are therapeutic beyond any advancements neuropsychology could ever offer.

ABOUT THE AUTHOR

 **DR. JULIE LOPEZ** began her professional career as a system engineer, drawn to the challenge and complexity of the field, but ultimately found her passion for systems lay elsewhere. She was drawn to work with an infinitely more complicated system, our human system.

The change in direction led her to study the effects of trauma on our system and to work at the DC Rape Crisis Center while building a private clinical practice and establishing a comprehensive mental health program for immigrants that earned her the honor of Social Worker of the Year 2001 by the DC Metro Chapter of the National Association of Social Workers.

Dr. Julie taught as an adjunct professor for almost a decade at the Catholic University of America before founding the Viva Center (www.vivapartnership.com), a visionary mental health center specializing in advanced brain- and body-based therapies and a trauma-informed approach to healing. Her center houses over twenty-five practitioners, all of them deeply committed to the diversity of healing modalities and the complexity of effective care that is unique for each human system.

With profits from the center and a strong commitment to destigmatizing mental health, as well as empowerment of the community, the Viva leadership team elected to launch a free online mental health resource called the Resilient Brain Project (https://resilientbrainproject.com). This one-stop-shop mental health repository offers resources like apps, support forums, and empowering knowledge on how our human system can be changed. Also included is information for allies: friends, family, or teachers.

Dr. Julie has been featured in many news outlets and in the court system as a trauma expert (www.drjulielopez.com). She runs a postgraduate training program on trauma-informed clinical practice and enjoys speaking, retreat and forum facilitation, as well as conducting trainings on how to empower lives, especially those impacted by adoption.